Red Legs of the Bulge

Artillerymen in the Battle of the Bulge

C.J. Kelly

WORLD WAR II HISTORY 3
BENNINGTON, VERMONT
2014

First Edition published in 2014 by the Merriam Press

First Edition

ISBN 9781500497088
Library of Congress Control Number 2014945803
Merriam Press #WH3-P

This work was designed, produced, and published in
the United States of America by the

Merriam Press
133 Elm Street Suite 3R
Bennington VT 05201

E-mail: ray@merriam-press.com
Web site: merriam-press.com

The Merriam Press publishes new manuscripts on historical subjects, especially military history and with an emphasis on World War II, as well as reprinting previously published works, including reports, documents, manuals, articles and other materials on historical topics.

THE term 'Red Legs' for members of the Field Artillery Branch goes back to the American Civil War, when the soldiers manning the guns began wearing red piping on their pants in order to distinguish themselves from their infantry brethren.

Author's Note

I have chosen to use the word Colored and Negro interchangeably as opposed to the more socially acceptable African-American. Although repugnant to us today, this was the language in use during the war and how the segregated units were officially designated. It is important to use the vernacular of the times about which I am writing. This is not only historically accurate but brings home the reality of the lives of African American troops and the indignities they had to overcome.

Dialogue in certain chapters has been reconstructed from personal interviews, memoirs, journals and letters. The passage of time has left room for omission and errors. Therefore, the dialogue is not a verbatim transcript, but how the men remember it.

Contents

Acknowledgments

THIS work would not have been possible without the help of many individuals. I wish to gratefully acknowledge the assistance given by John Kline, John Gatens, John Schaffner, Richard Ferguson, Jack Roberts, the late E.V. Creel and the entire 106th Division Association. Author Dr. Norman Lichtenfeld was an invaluable source of information on the 333rd. Big thanks to my point man in the Ardennes, researcher Carl Wouters. To Lynn Simpkins, who patiently explained the English language to me and helped me through my comma addiction; Tom Houlihan, mapmaker extraordinaire and editor; Devin McGinley of the Fair Lawn Patch, and finally, to my wife Ann, for her patience and understanding.

"Leave the Artillerymen alone, they are an obstinate lot..."
—Napoleon Bonaparte

Preface

PEOPLE often ask me why I have an ardent interest in World War II. Well, that answer is easy: I'm the son of a World War II veteran and the nephew of six others. These men were around me all the time growing up. My world view was formed from being in their company. They were tough guys with a heart, and I got to know the real men who lived the lives depicted in the movies. My Bronx neighborhood was filled with patriotic veterans from every war of the 20th century. We also had numerous Holocaust survivors. One day at the grocery store, I remember asking my mother why the three men who owned the place had tattooed numbers on their forearms. Every time they handed a patron change, you could not miss the fading black-inked numbers.

Another questions I'm often asked just as often: Why the fascination with the Battle of the Bulge? I had an uncle who served in the battle. He was a decorated officer in the military police, but passed away before I knew him. So that was not a factor. Watching documentaries as a kid, particularly *The World at War* and seeing the newsreel footage of American Prisoners of War in Europe was rather shocking. This piqued my curiosity. My father's experiences had been horrible. He survived North Africa, Sicily and the campaign across France. Those campaigns all ended up being regarded as great victories. He was rotated off the line in September, and spared the Allies' stalled offensives throughout the fall of 1944, the nightmare of the Hürtgen Forest and the physical ordeal of the winter campaign. So his stories tended to point out the positives. Near the end of his life, he finally began to speak about his friends who died, and some of the other horrors.

In the late 1990s, I began seeking out the memoirs of the men who fought in the battle. This coincided with a flood of books that were published. These shed light on the soldiers' experiences on both sides of the conflict. No less important was the World Wide Web in increasing access to veterans' stories. Through the internet, I was able to find a variety of resources. I wanted to find the men who were in those newsreels. Most of those men in the famous German propaganda footage that I saw were from the 106th infantry division, who held out for four days in terrible conditions, and although suffering grievous losses, ultimately upset the Nazis' timetable for conquest. Upon reading Gerald Astor's *A Blood Dimmed Tide* and Michael Tolhurst's *St. Vith*, my obsession began anew, and I sought out those veterans in order to write a novel based on their experiences. It was nice to reconnect with members of that generation so soon after the passing of my dad and uncles.

While I was piecing together their stories for my novel, which deals with the escape of two artillerymen from the Germans, I felt compelled to learn as much as I could about artillery operations during the war and the daily life of an artilleryman in Northwest Europe. The Artillery Branch is one of the most complicated of military science. Being an artillery officer in the United States Army, just as in many other armies, was a highly treasured commission. Like the Engineers, it was a technically demanding field; only the top graduates of military schools or ROTC usually received the appointments. All of the enlisted complements were highly skilled as well. They had to be able learn such things as surveying, radio communications and gun mechanics.

During the war, recruits felt lucky to be assigned to the artillery. They figured it was safer than the infantry. With the exception of being a forward observer, they were correct. Although making up 16% of an infantry division's strength, it only accounted for 3% of the casualties.[1] By contrast, an infantryman's chances of making it through the war unscathed, especially in a rifle company, were slim. In the European Theater of Operations (ETO), the average lifespan of a company commander was two weeks. Most rifle companies turned over their personnel two or three times before the end of the war. Consequently, the foot soldier thought anyone in the artillery lived a life of relative luxury. That situation changed during the Bulge. It was no longer a safe billet. Battery personnel were some of the first to get hit by enemy shells. The front line came to them as never before. German infantry and tanks bypassed the infantry screen and rolled up on their positions. In an age of indirect fire and advanced observation techniques, direct fire on a target became commonplace. Others, fighting with carbines and bazookas, held off many a thrust by the enemy, some even fighting hand to hand. Desperate men had to call down fire on their own positions to help stave off oncoming Panzers.

Recognition has not always come. Other than Napoleon, can the

---

[1]   Michael D. Doubler, *Closing with the Enemy* (Lawrence, Kansas: University of Kansas Press, 1994), 240.

average person name a famous artilleryman? The answer is probably not. There are examples in U.S. military history where artillery has received some lasting acclaim: Taylor's guns at Buena Vista, the Civil War battles of Malvern Hill or Stones River. Pershing's guns played a major role in the victories at Belleau Wood and the Meuse Argonne. During World War II, Ernie Pyle devoted a whole chapter on a battery from the Italian Front in his work *Brave Men*. That was a rare treat. Cannoneers, fire direction centers, and artillery observers bracketing fire on targets are usually not fodder for books or movies. Nevertheless, their contributions to the final victory were enormous. Patton, the tanker, often commented that our artillery won the war.

The use of artillery reached its zenith in World War II. It accounted for the majority of casualties on the battlefield. The U.S. Army led the way in both gun design and the development of advanced observation techniques taught at places like Fort Sill, Oklahoma. All this innovation came to fruition during the last year of the war with the ability to concentrate firepower on the enemy through the use of combined arms techniques honed in the hedgerows of Normandy. The weather in Northern Europe by December 1944 was atrocious, nullifying the Allies' air superiority. So the artillery had to fill that void. During the first week of the Battle, the U.S. Army was able to amass almost 350 guns of all calibers, one of the largest concentrations in the history of warfare, to defend the Elsenborn Ridge in the northern sector of the Bulge. The Sixth SS Panzer Army literally ran into a wall of steel. Throughout the rest of the campaign, artillery continued to be penultimate battlefield weapon. At Bastogne, standing right alongside the 101st Airborne were Red Legs, many of them African-American.

American dominance in field artillery would continue until the end of the war. However, with the ascendency of military aviation, the branch would increasingly take a backseat in the coming years. This was interrupted only by the Korean conflict, which is often called the artilleryman's war because of the mountain top duels that often lasted for days.

My research led me in many directions. In the end I was left with a mountain of personal memoirs, books, after-action reports, photos, and 1940s artillery manuals. I had learned about the minutest details of artillery battalion operations: from being a gunner, a forward observer, or a technician at the fire direction center. After I completed *The Lion's Path*, my passion was not quenched. I still wanted to educate others. So I came upon the idea for a non-fiction work that would encapsulate my research and pay tribute to the veterans who inspired the novel's characters. Through these efforts, I hope to play a small role in keeping this knowledge alive for future generations.

This work focuses on a small, but very important part of the larger battle in and around St. Vith, highlighting the artillery units from the 106th infantry division as well as the 333rd Field Artillery. It tells the story from the artillerymen's point of view. In that sense, I hope it sheds light on some untold aspects of the war and leads others to seek out further information about the conflict.

Introduction

IN the late summer and early fall of 1944, there was a confidence among the Western Allies that bordered on hubris. With the Russians moving in from the East, Germany was being squeezed on two fronts. There was even talk of victory by Christmas. Some top commanders were placing friendly wagers amongst themselves on what date the war would end.

Within weeks, those attitudes began to change as harbingers of trouble emerged. Operation Market Garden, Montgomery's attempt at the end of September to dash across the Rhine in Holland, ended in almost the total annihilation of the British 1st Airborne at Arnhem. Later that fall, Allied forces failed to secure the vital approaches to the port of Antwerp until November. That caused vast delays in supplying the Western Armies who were approaching Germany. In September, poor intelligence led American commanders to launch an attack through the rugged, dense *Hürtgen Forest* on the border of Germany. The assault chewed up five American divisions in close quarters fighting that would be replayed in Vietnam twenty years later. Ground had to be retaken again and again. The campaign's goal was seemingly undefined. It would end in a bloody stalemate three months later. With the Germans now fighting on their own soil, the Siegfried Line was proving to be a formidable barrier.

In addition, there was the conflict between Allied commanders. General Dwight D. Eisenhower had been trying to keep the peace between his principal commanders, British General Montgomery and American Omar Bradley. This tension was further heightened by the machinations of General George Patton, commander of the American Third Army, and a long-time Montgomery antagonist. Each general had their own view of how the war should be won. They fought each other almost as hard they fought the Germans.

The ever cautious Montgomery favored a single thrust strategy. This meant leveling a large force against a specific point in the front, with his 21st Army Group in the lead, of course. The rest of the Allied forces were there to guard his flank. Eisenhower wanted a broad front strategy. This involved keeping constant pressure on the Germans all along the Western front from Southern France to Holland. One could liken this to a battle of attrition in which you wear down your enemy so much that by the time the big blow arrives, they are exhausted. Both ideas had their merits, though Ike won out.

The broad front method had one glaring problem: supplies. Having your armies spread along the German frontier from the south of France to the North Sea caused excessive delays. Due to the lack of deep water ports, most supplies were still trucked to the front over unreliable roads from temporary harbors or beaches. Allied forces had outrun their supply lines. The City of Antwerp and its large port had been seized in September, but the approaches to the port, down the Schelde Estuary, were still held by the Germans. The French port of Cherbourg was still being repaired and had limited operations. Some port cities, such as Lorient, were holding out against the Allies, while others were just too small to handle the increased shipping. Shortages in ammunition and food began taking its toll on the men at the front as priorities were changed almost daily.

The high casualty rates suffered since the landing in Normandy on June 6, 1944 surprised the Western Allies. The amphibious assault was expected to be tough, but it was the prolonged, brutal fighting in the hedgerow country throughout June and July that came as a shock. The Germans' tenacious defense held off the Allies for almost two months before Paris was finally taken. Even with a 3 to 1 advantage in men and materiel, offensive operations began to bog down as summer turned to fall. Control of the skies had long since been wrested from the Luftwaffe. Years of bombing Germany's industrial areas should have destroyed its ability to make war. Still, the Germans continued to fight. German industrial output actually increased in 1943 and 1944. As a result of this miscalculation, a manpower shortage developed. Many American divisions still training in the states were stripped of their experienced personnel, taken as replacements for units decimated after Normandy. New recruits had been rushed through basic training and were going to have to learn on the job. In many cases, they died trying. Large numbers of African-American units were finally being put into action. Previously relegated to support roles, they were now represented in all branches of the Army. The 333rd and 969th field artillery battalions along with the 761st Tank Battalion, also known as "Patton's Panthers," were just some of those *Negro* units beginning to see combat.

By December, the front was static; winter weather had arrived. The Germans dug in along the remaining barriers of the Siegfried line and waited for the big blow to arrive, most likely in the Ruhr, the industrial heartland of the Reich. The Allied victories of the summer and early fall were distant memories, and the war had become a slow battle of attrition against an increasingly desperate enemy. So along this "ghost front," as it was now being called, things became routine. Rumors about Glen Miller appearing in Paris were heard everywhere. Marlene Dietrich and Dinah Shore were coming too. Ernie Pyle left for the Pacific. If the action-seeking reporters had left, there might not be much to do for a while; the Germans, with no real diversions of any kind, kept themselves busy preparing fortified positions that the Allies would have to overcome.

Against this backdrop, the 106th Infantry Division arrived on the continent. They eventually made their way to the Schnee Eifel region on the eastern edge of the Ardennes Forest, a rugged, hilly region in the tri-border area of Belgium, Germany and Luxembourg. The area had a Christmas card look with its narrow winding roads, and mist-shrouded, snowy hills, interspersed with dense forests of fir and pine. The locals in their area, mostly of German descent with a sprinkling of French speaking and Flemish Belgians, were indifferent at best. The ethnic mix brought on overlapping loyalties during the war.

The Division was made up of three infantry regiments, three 105mm artillery battalions and one heavy 155mm battalion, along with various other support units. It was formed in March 1943 and spent 18 months getting ready to go overseas. Not only did the enlisted men lack any combat experience, but most of its officers did as well. Even General Alan W. Jones, the division commander, had never heard a shot fired in anger; neither had Eisenhower for that matter. The Golden Lions, as men of the Division were known because of their shoulder patch which featured a golden lion's face encircled by red, white and blue borders, spent the winter training in the mountains of Tennessee and the summer of 1944 sweltering at Camp Atterbury, Indiana. Army brass assumed that if recruits received the toughest training the Army could offer, it would more than make up for any lack of experience. However, during that spring and summer, the Division lost almost 7,000 of its original enlisted complement to replacement depots, 60% of its enlisted strength.[2] With the invasion of continental Europe imminent, and the Army expecting high casualty rates during the first weeks of the invasion, almost every available Army unit waiting in the

---

[2]   Ernest R. Dupuy, *St. Vith: Lion in the Way* (Nashville: The Battery Press, 1986) 7.

States was stripped of personnel. New men were brought in, and commanders hurriedly tried to get them up to speed before deployment. But the new men had trained for a very different war. Men from the Army Specialized Training Program (ASTP) were some of the first to arrive. ASTP was a program that sent qualified men to college to eventually train for specialties the army would need later. Many of these men were surprised by their "reassignment." Other replacements came from the Army Air Corps and Army Ground Forces replacement depots. There were also volunteers from antiaircraft and coastal artillery units that were being disbanded along with a large contingent of service troops (supply units mostly) and military police.[3]

Once they arrived in Europe, the men were told there would have time to get acclimated to combat conditions. The Ardennes was supposed to be sparsely defended by enemy units made up of old men and others ill-suited for combat. The Division's area of responsibility covered over twenty miles, well beyond what Army regulations stated for a division. Two thirds of the division would be located inside the German border. Despite this fact, the men of the 2nd Infantry Division, whom they were replacing, joked that the new guys were going to have it easy.

Traveling to the front had been a cold and miserable journey. A driving rain fell. Ice and mud impeded the drive. And it was not without incident; there had been one casualty from a weather-related traffic accident. Warrant Officer Claude Collins of the 590th Field Artillery was hit by a truck and killed. Reaching the Schnee Eifel was a relief. Many of the men were billeted in farmhouses or log cabins that had been built by the previous GIs. Even with the cold and snow, morale was high. By 1700 on the evening of December 9, 1944, registration by the artillery battalions was complete. Some batteries even fired a few harassing rounds at the enemy, which was part of a regular program of unobserved fire missions started by the 2nd Infantry Division.[4]

So all along the front things were expected to stay quiet. The first few days were routine for the men. Patrols were sent out. Artillery batteries had a few more fire missions, mostly unobserved due to the weather. The enemy shot a few flares and lobbed some shells that missed, but that was about it. There were some mishaps: fires broke out at a company kitchen and one of the regimental command posts;

---

[3] *Ibid.*, 7.
[4] *Ibid.*, 13.

most likely due to carelessness rather than any enemy sabotage. Strangely, it elicited no fire from the enemy. Rumors ran rampant about Germans infiltrating at night. Engine noise coming from the German side of the line increased each day, which added to their general unease. As the days passed, the whistle of steam locomotives across the Prum Valley was heard with increasing frequency. Within the higher command structure, no one appeared concerned even after German recon planes were heard flying over their positions. Any concerns sent up the intelligence chain by the 106th were chalked up to nerves by the VIII Corps G-2. The fears were met with much derision by the Corps intelligence staff who scoffed at the new arrivals' reports. Intelligence officers told the 106th's infantry units that the Germans were playing recorded sounds of tanks and other vehicles to scare the newcomers.[5]

The sounds were all too real. Hitler had three armies massing in the Ardennes: the newly formed Sixth SS Panzer Army in the north, led by Hitler's close confidant, General Sepp Dietrich, which had almost 500 tanks and self-propelled guns; the Fifth Panzer Army, headed by General Hasso von Manteuffel; and furthest south, the Seventh Army, made up of mostly infantry units. These combined Armies contained almost 30 infantry divisions and 12 Panzer divisions. The goal was to split the Allied armies, and retake Antwerp. The Fifth Panzer was given the job of cutting through the long, thin front held by the 106th in the St. Vith sector.[6]

The Battle of the Bulge, so named because of the salient the attack caused in the American line, became the biggest and bloodiest battle that the U.S. fought in World War II. Over a million men were joined in the fight which officially lasted six weeks. The Americans contributed 600,000 GIs and suffered over 80,000 casualties. The Germans were thought to have suffered nearly 100,000 dead, wounded and captured.[7] Most historians believe the battle hastened the end of the war because Germany leapt from behind its Siegfried Line and took casualties it could ill afford. Most importantly, it shook the Allied High Command from an embarrassing complacency and forced American commanders to improvise new methods of fighting in a deadly form of on-the-job training.

---

[5]   *Ibid.*, 18.
[6]   Charles B. MacDonald, *A Time for Trumpets: The Untold Story of the Battle of the Bulge* (New York: William Morrow and Company Inc., 1985) 29.
[7]   *Ibid.*, 618.

In the early stages of the Battle of the Bulge, artillery units proved invaluable in slowing the German offensive. Recovering from the initial shock, men ran to their guns and often stayed there until ordered out, or in some cases, until they were killed. The speed and accuracy with which the American guns fired astonished the Germans. Caught on the muddy roads and deep ravines of the Ardennes, the German attacks were finally stopped cold by the sheer massing of firepower. Many stunned German POWs would often ask their American captors if they could see the "automatic" guns that had bombarded them. They could not imagine that so much firepower could be brought to bear through just sheer human effort and planning. After the war, when the U.S. Army conducted studies on the effectiveness of their efforts throughout every branch, it was the artillery branch that received the highest marks time and time again. Unlike other branches, the groundwork for success was laid out long before Pearl Harbor. The infantry and armored branches had to learn on the job, suffering defeats and high casualties before developing new techniques to replace the outmoded ones they had been taught in the states. For the artillerymen, it was different. They hit the ground running in 1942 because their success was twenty years in the making.

During the interwar years, the United States became a deeply isolationist nation. Even with its military triumphs during World War I and its ascendancy onto the world stage, the United States downsized its army. In the midst of an economic boom during the 1920s, government spending was slashed, in particular, the budgets of both main services. For some Army officers, ranks were frozen. Others reverted back to a former rank. With the coming of the Great Depression, the cutbacks became worse. By 1939, the regular Army numbered less than 200,000 men making it only the 17th largest in the world.[8] But that did not stop the Army from experimenting in new technology and tactics. There were still dedicated men in the service that had foresight and a passion to innovate. Nowhere was this more evident than at Fort Sill, Oklahoma, home of the U.S. Army's artillery branch. Under the direction of men such as Carlos Brewer, Leslie McNair, Jacob Devers and Orlando Ward, all of whom would serve as generals in World War II, modern artillery practices were born. Many of the new develop-

---

[8] Rick Atkinson, *An Army at Dawn: The War in North Africa, 1942-1943* (New York: Owl Books, 2003) 8.

ments had started with the British, but the Americans took the ideas and developed them into a unified system.

As late as the 1930s, much of the artillery was still horse drawn. Military theorists knew this had to change. Mobility and adaptability on the battlefield were going to be the keys to successful military operations in the future. When he became Army Chief of Staff in the early '30s, General Douglas MacArthur ordered the branch to motorize.[9] Tractors and trucks became the new mode of transport. Throughout the decade, new, larger weapons were tested, and old ones improved. New methods for amassing fires on targets, such as *Time on Target* missions, were developed. The idea of a centralized artillery command and control system along with the concept of non-divisional artillery battalions took shape. These innovations helped create a system that was second to none during World War II.

The Fire Direction Center (FDC) was developed between 1932 and 1934. The centers centralized the computing of firing data within the battalion. Not only did this allow gunners to mass fire rapidly, it changed the role of the battalion. Prior to this time, battery commanders acted almost autonomously, directing their own fire while battalion commanders were more like administrators, parceling out assignments and supervising ammunition supply. Now, the battalion commander assumed responsibility for fire direction and the battery commander would conduct the fire. During operations, the battalion CO would dispatch officers who acted as forward observers (FOs) from the batteries and/or battalion. The observers would report their targeting information back to the centers by radio instead of telephone, although the latter would be used extensively throughout the war as well. The center would then prepare firing data, apply the necessary corrections and make the adjustments in order to synchronize fire on the most important targets. This innovation allowed a battalion to shift fire rapidly and mass it on a single target.[10]

Similar operations existed not only at the Battalion level, but at various stages within the command structure. This gave American observers options, which was vital in the heat of battle. Forward observers from a particular battery could call up their divisional artillery cen-

---

[9]   Boyd L. Dastrup, *King of Battle: A Branch History of the U.S. Army's Field Artillery* (Office of the Command Historian, United States Army Training and Doctrine Command, Fort Monroe, Virginia and the Center of Military History, United State Army, Washington, D.C. 1993) 192.

[10] *Ibid.*, 197-198.

ter or even a Corps unit to get a fire mission. All of those units had personnel capable of completing a fire mission. Also, calling a battery HQ directly and bypassing the Battalion center became commonplace in the first days of the Bulge. Although a firing battery usually received its firing orders from the battalion FDC, and would not have a complete set of FDC personnel, it had a firing officer and a communications specialist to aid an observer who desperately needed a fire mission.

Communication was the key to the entire system, which was not an easy task under combat conditions. If an infantry platoon leader was calling for fire, he was probably under severe pressure and would get priority. Besides the EE8A telephones and the SCR 610 radios carried by all forward observation teams, the Army gave every infantry unit, regardless of its size, a radio as well. The nation's industrial capacity made this possible. U.S. companies were able to produce a multitude of different radios and the dry cell batteries the Army required at a staggering rate. So in addition to the forward observers, any infantry platoon or squad leader could call in a fire mission to a battalion FDC or battery HQ by using an SCR-536 radio, a grid map and compass. The SCR-536s are better known today as "walkie talkies." By war's end, over 100,000 SCR-536s were produced.

At the FDCs, the observer's request was converted into proper firing commands for the gun crews. Officers in the Fire Direction Center sifted through all the calls for help and decided how much support to assign to each mission request, given the observer's position, the probable target, weather and the ammunition restrictions. FDC personnel used such things as pre-computed graphical firing tables with a set of clear protractors and rulers already corrected for wind, powder, etc. The tables were basically large books of logarithmic calculations that were created for all manner of distances.[11] So converging the sheaf was possible, with a response time that was not only quick and for the most part, amazingly accurate.[12]

During the war, a typical fire mission started with an urgent call from a forward observer, such as "Crow, this is Crow Baker 3. Fire Mission. Enemy infantry." In this instance, "Crow" stood for the Battalion, "Baker" indicating they were from B Battery, and "3" was the

---

[11] David T. Zabecki, *World War II in Europe: An Encyclopedia* (New York & London: Garland Publishing, Inc. 1999) 825-827.

[12] Bernard Thielen, Lt., "Practical Method for Converging the Sheaf," *Field Artillery Journal*, Vol. 29, No. 2, Fort Sill, OK, March/April 1939: 126.

number of the observation team.[13] Identifying the target, such as infantry, helped determine the type of shell used. A high explosive round (HE) was usually used against personnel because it would explode prior to impact, thereby scattering the fragments along a fifty to one hundred yard area (for a 105mm). The observer's primary tool was his BC ("Battalion Commander's) scope. It was usually mounted on a tripod, and contained a graduated reticule in its focal plane, similar to a crosshair in a rifle scope, which helped the observers measure horizontal and vertical angles.

Upon confirmation, the orders were relayed to the firing battery (or multiple batteries if necessary): *"Battery Adjust, Shell HE, Fuse quick, Base Deflection right 250 mils, Elevation 1150, One round to adjust – number one gun only."* Then after a slight pause, he gave the command, "Fire!" Only one gun would fire until the adjustments on the target had been completed. The observers were then told *"on the way."* Adjustments were made by the observers until the target was fully bracketed. So orders from the FOs such as *"up 100"* or *"100 over"* were commonplace after the initial volley. Once the observer was satisfied that the target was properly bracketed, an order for *"Fire for Effect!"* would follow. The guns assigned to that particular mission would then all open up on the target. The actual amount of shells fired varied per mission though a volley of three shots per gun was standard during the initial fire mission.[14]

This is not to say the system was perfect. Errors were made that cost lives. Friendly fire was a real problem throughout the war. Weather and technical problems plagued the communication system. Having to read a map and call out orders under fire was a daunting task that caused a breakdown in the skills taught back in the states. Observation teams traveled with the infantry. Like the foot soldiers, they experienced the deprivations and mental anguish of men under constant threat. The artillery forward observer's lifespan was measured in weeks.

The FDC personnel were also under immense pressure. The centers themselves were bustling, sometimes chaotic places, crowded with dozens of personnel hovering over makeshift wooden tables that were covered with maps and other data. Phones rang and radios buzzed. Cigarette smoke filled the air. Tense officers peered over the shoulders

---

[13] Robert Weiss, *Enemy North, South, East, West* (Portland, OR: Strawberry Hill Press, 1998) 46.

[14] Robert C. Baldridge, *Victory Road* (1st Books, 2003) 89-90.

of their enlisted technicians as the calls came in. Split-second decisions had to be made. Data was checked and rechecked until final approval of a target was given. The training was incredibly rigorous for everyone involved, sometimes lasting up to two years. Without that training and strict adherence to protocol, friendly-fire casualty rates would have been much higher.

Weapons evolved as well during the pre-war period. The towed 105mm and 155mm howitzers, which were standard issue by the late '30s, were improved but the Army continued testing even after Pearl Harbor. Materials and maintenance were constantly evaluated. As always, it was the seemingly simple changes that made a big difference. Innovations, like pneumatic tires, were used for the first time in 1942, which replaced the solid rubber ones. This made transport much easier and there was less wear and tear on the gun carriage.

When the Americans saw the success of the German armored forces in the first two years of the war rampaging across Europe, the development of self-propelled artillery became an imperative. They needed weapons that could to keep up with the tanks of the new armored divisions. Finding the right chassis for both the 105mm and 155mm was the biggest problem. A 105mm mobile platform was developed in time for use in the North African campaign and it would go on to be one of most successful weapons in the American inventory. Development of a self-propelled 155mm took much longer. They did not begin arriving in Europe until the fall of 1944, and in much lesser numbers than the 105mm. All of the self-propelled 155mm battalions were Corps units and used in various artillery groups.

Just prior for the outbreak of the war, a system of aerial forward observation was established. This was the penultimate development for the branch, and helped the Americans become masters of combined arms tactics. It took a long intra-service fight. The Artillery hierarchy wanted their own planes and to have them under the control of the Battalion or Corps commander. Predictably, the Air Corps was incensed, wanting control of all air assets. The Artillerymen prevailed. The little Piper Cubs that the battalions used, known officially as the "L-4," became a symbol of impending doom for many German troops. [15] Enemy soldiers knew if they could see one in the sky, their position had been targeted and it would be only a matter of minutes before a rain of steel would come down. Time and time again in post-

---

[15]   Dastrup, *op.cit.*, 206-207.

war interrogations, German soldiers mentioned seeing those planes and the fear they engendered.

THE WEAPONS

The two primary pieces used by American artillery battalions in World War II were the 105mm howitzer (M2A1) and 155mm howitzer. The triangular structure of the World War II infantry division called for three battalions of 105mm supporting each of the three infantry regiments of the division and one heavy battalion of 155mm howitzers, which was used at the discretion of the Division artillery commander.[16]

The 105mm M2A1, along with its many variants, was the most widely used light artillery piece in the American inventory. Between 1941 and 1945, 8,536 were produced. Based on a German design, it was developed after World War I. By 1941, it had replaced the 75mm field gun as standard issue.[17] Twenty percent of all the shells fired by the US during the war were 105mm high explosive rounds.[18] When fully charged, it fired a 33 pound shell, had a range of approximately seven miles, and one shell burst could cover 50 yards or more. It required a crew of nine men, although in combat this varied, with sometimes seven having to suffice during fire missions. The primary shells were high explosive (HE), armor piercing (HEAT) and smoke, which was primarily white phosphorus. There were various fuses. For HE rounds, these included *point-detonating,* or *time and superquick.*[19] During the last six months of the war in Europe, the proximity fuse or variable-time fuse was introduced. It carried a small radar device which would trigger detonation at a preset distance from a target. This greatly enhanced the use of air bursts against the enemy, which could spread deadly shrapnel over a larger surface area.[20]

---

[16] Zabecki, *op.cit.*, 826.

[17] Steven J. Zaloga, *US Field Artillery in World War II* (Oxford, UK, Osprey Publishing, 2007) 9-12.

[18] Kurt Laughlin and Tim Streeter, "105mm Howitzer Ammunition: Boxes, Bundles, Tubes and Rounds." usarmymodels.com, 2002-2007, 24 June 2012. http://www.usarmymodels.com/articles/105mm%20 Ordnance/1%2010.

[19] Field Manual, *FM 105-mm Howitzer M2 Questions and Answers.* Field Artillery School (July 1942).

[20] Dastrup, *op.cit.*, 225.

The 589th, 590th and 591st of the 106th ID each used the 105mm M2A1. The standard Army 2½ ton truck (6x6) acted as its prime mover.[21] The majority of 105mms were issued to organic battalions within a divisional structure, but there were some non-divisional 105mm M2 battalions that served in Europe during the last year of the war.

The Marine Corps, which used the 75mm howitzer as their standard piece, also adopted the 105mm as part of their artillery complement at the beginning of the war, although on a much more limited basis. A battalion of the 11th Marines was issued the 105mm and it was actually used as heavy artillery during the Guadalcanal campaign in 1942 until the 155mm units arrived. During the Battle of Bloody Ridge, several batteries of 105mm helped stemmed the tide of the battle by firing point blank into the Japanese infantry.[22]

Armored Field Artillery battalions used the self-propelled (SP) version of the gun. The 105mm Howitzer Motor Carriage M7, was laid out on what was formerly an M3 tank chassis. The self-propelled 105mm was finally accepted into service in early 1942 and was shipped to the British Eighth Army in North Africa for its baptism of fire. It proved its worth immediately during the Second Battle of El Alamein in October 1942. It became known as the *Priest*; so named because of the pulpit-like structure on its right front side. The *Priest* served in all of the American armored divisions. Over 4,000 were produced during the war and it also saw service during the Korean War.[23]

The 105mm had a short-nosed variant known as the M3, which was used in cannon companies and some airborne units. Cannon companies were organic to all infantry regiments and were under the direct control of the regimental commander. By 1944, the standard cannon company had three platoons with two 105 M3s along with a variety of other heavy small arms. The units were supposed to provide supplemental fire support for the regiment. Tactically, they never quite worked as intended, and were disbanded after the war, although the M3 continued in service for some time. Later in the war, many airborne artillery units that had been using the 75mm pack howitzer, converted to the M3 105mm.[24]

The 155mm howitzer was used as both divisional and non-

---

[21] Zaloga, *op.cit.*, 39.

[22] Henry I. Shaw, *First Offensive: The Marine Campaign for Guadalcanal* (Ann Arbor: University of Michigan Press, 1992) 12; 25-27.

[23] Zaloga, *op.cit.*, 41-42.

[24] *Ibid.*, 13-14.

divisional artillery. In the 106th, it was used by the 592nd and also by the non-divisional 333rd. It fired a 95 pound shell, and had a range of 9 miles. A crew of 11 was required. It was normally towed by an M5 HST tractor. There was a variant of the 155mm called the *Long Tom*, used by non-divisional/Corps artillery units. The nickname came from its longer barrel that required a different carriage. It was truck-towed using the Mack 7½-ton 6x6 truck until the M4 HST tractor became available.[25] There were two self-propelled versions using a 155mm, the M12 and the M40. The M12 used the French World War I 155mm GPF, and was mounted on the M3 tank chassis. Officially, it was known as the 155mm Gun Motor Carriage M12. Even though it used the same chassis as the self-propelled 105mm, weight and recoil problems caused delays in production. But when finally deployed in late 1944, it proved its worth and became an invaluable part of the Allied arsenal. The 155mm Gun Motor Carriage M40 used the 155mm Long Tom and was mounted on the M4A3 medium tank chassis. It did not reach the European Theatre until 1945.

Other artillery pieces that were used extensively throughout the war were the 8-inch and 240mm howitzers as well as the 75mm pack howitzer (Marine and Airborne units). The former two were strictly used within the non-divisional framework. A 4.5-inch gun was also part of the American arsenal but in relatively small numbers. The gun was mounted on a 155mm howitzer carriage, and despite having a smaller barrel, it had a longer range and bested its 155mm cousin by 3 miles. Never produced in sufficient quantities to make a significant impact, it was discontinued right after the war. The remaining guns were shipped to Fort Sill to be used for training.[26]

In terms of their individual small arms, all the artillerymen were issued the standard M1 Carbine. Carbines were semi-automatic, but much lighter than the infantry's M1 Garands, which made it one of the most widely used small arms of the war. Additionally, noncoms and officers carried a .45 caliber pistol as a sidearm. The battery's other small arms amounted to two .50 caliber machine guns, and at least one bazooka. On rare occasions, an officer or noncom might get his hands on a Thompson submachine gun or M1 Garand, but they were exceptions.

---

[25] *Ibid.*, 22.
[26] *Ibid.*, 18-19.

THE ARTILLERY BATTALION

The size of the battalion depended on its main weapon. The bigger the gun, the more men you needed, though the basic battalion structure for both the 105mm M2A1 and 155mm M1A1 unit was similar regardless of the gun. Each battalion had three firing batteries (4 guns each), a Headquarters battery (the CO and his staff along with the fire direction personnel, communications center, etc.), and a Service battery (ammunition, basic supplies, mechanics, etc.). Batteries were further subdivided into sections. Battalions were usually headed by a lieutenant colonel with an executive officer who was usually a major. Batteries were headed by a captain with an exec who was a lieutenant. A 105mm battalion contained just over 500 men. Each battery had about 100 men, which broke down into five officers and 95 enlisted of various rank. A 155mm battalion had approximately 550 enlisted men with 30 officers, with each battery having around 120 men.[27] Once combat operations began however, it was rare for any unit at any level (Division, Battalion, Regimental, etc.) to have a complete table of organization. There was a replacement system, but the exigencies of combat left all units in the combat arms (infantry, armor, engineer or artillery) short of men. The Battle of the Bulge caused such a manpower crisis in infantry units that even some artillery units ended up sending non-essential personnel to the infantry as replacements.

Within an infantry division, each 105mm battalion was assigned an infantry regiment to support, forming a combat team. The assignments were made back in the States and continued upon deployment. In the 106th, the 589th was assigned to the 422nd Infantry Regiment, the 590th to the 423rd, and the 591st supported the 424th. The 155mm battalion supported the units or areas most in need at the discretion of Division command. Besides the four firing battalions, the 106th's artillery complement also contained a Division Headquarters component. It consisted of a battery headquarters, operations platoon, communication platoon, an air observation section and a maintenance section. Included in the operations platoon was an instrument and survey section along with a meteorological section. The communications platoon had the wire and radio section which was provided with over 30 miles of tele-

---

[27] Field Artillery School Instruction Memorandum T-1, *Organization of Field Artillery of the Infantry Division and Employment of the Field Artillery Battalion in Reconnaissance, Selection and Occupation of Position* (Fort Sill, Oklahoma: Printing Plant Field Artillery School, 1942), 14-17.

RED LEGS OF THE BULGE

phone wire and 4 radio sets. The supply and cooks sections rounded out the unit. [28]

The jobs of the enlisted members of each firing battery varied depending on their training and circumstances with many personnel being cross-trained to do a variety of work. Each gun crew was considered a section and within each section there was a sergeant (Section Chief), a gunner corporal and assistant gunner (known as the *#1*), two other assistant gunners and three cannoneers. A driver and assistant driver rounded out the 105mm section, making for a total of nine men. [29] Although requiring more personnel and having some technical differences, the duties of the 155mm crews were essentially the same.

Behind the safety plate, on the left side of the breech, the gunner corporal worked a telescopic sight known as the gunner's quadrant (or gunner's scope), containing an azimuth scale that measured horizontal deflection, which he set on orders from the firing officer. Officially, it was called the M12A2 panoramic telescope. It could be rotated manually 360 degrees. The sight had an alcohol bubble which he had to level prior to firing while using a numbered wheel to traverse the tube left or right. Red and white aiming posts were laid to the rear of the sight, almost in a straight line. One aiming stake was approximately 30 to 40 yards back while another was placed halfway between the gun sight and the other stake. The position of aiming posts could vary depending on the unit and terrain. Upon receiving the orders from the firing officer such as *Command Left 10* or *Right 20*, the key task for the gunner was to get the aiming stakes and the gun sight lined up on the vertical crosshair in the scope. If the command was left 10, the head of the site would then be moved off of the aiming stakes by that many degrees. Then he would use a hand wheel to traverse the gun left. Looking through the sight once again to determine that he was still lined up with the aiming stakes, his last task would be to level the bubble, and shout 'Ready!' This told the Section Chief that the gun was ready to fire; he then held up his right arm as a signal to the gun crew. Keeping the gun aligned properly was a difficult task when under the pressure of multiple fire missions, so the gunners had ways of cheating a little bit. Where possible, they could set the scope on a fixed target (e.g. Church steeple) and line up the angle on that. The wide dispersal of an exploding shell, which could be more than 50 yards, gave the gunners

---

[28] *Ibid.*, 3-5
[29] *Ibid.*, 14-17, and John Gatens, Email to author, 7 April 2010.

room to be off a little bit.[30]

While the gunner corporal worked his sight, the assistant gunner, positioned on the right side of the breech, operated a hand wheel to set the elevation. During the relay of firing commands, included were terms such as *Up 15 or Down 5*, from the zero. Once the orders were received, he would spin his wheel to the correct angle. But his task did not end there; he also operated the breech block, set the primer and pulled the lanyard upon the order, *Fire!* Both he and the gunner corporal were also responsible for keeping the crew away from the tremendous recoil of the barrel which could kill or maim, especially in the 155mm. After firing, the breech was opened by the #1 and the shell casing would drop out automatically, where it was picked up by one of the loaders to be tossed aside.[31]

The two assistant gunners and three other cannoneers in the section were responsible for packing the shells with powder bags, setting the fuses according to the mission specifics and loading the shell. Although the shells were shipped semi-fixed with the fuse already installed, it was the powder that provided the punch, so that had to be added to the shell. Each shell could take up to seven bags of powder, which were wrapped in silk and tied together.[32] Maximum range for the 105mm was approximately seven miles (12,205 yds).[33] The ammo men would disassemble the shell, pack the bags based on the firing orders, and reattach the fuse. Then the fuse had to be set using a special wrench. The majority of the shells expended during fire missions were usually high explosive (HE). There was a setting sleeve located at the base of each fuse. On an HE round, the ammunition crews could set it for either *point detonating* (PD) or *time superquick* (TSQ). This depended on how it was turned. For example, if the setting sleeve was turned parallel to the shell, it was set for *superquick*.[34] Under the pressure of a fire mission, these tasks were hellish in the freezing, wet weather of Northern Europe. If your frostbitten hands were not already cut up from separating the silk powder bags with a knife, you

30 John Gatens, Email to author, 10 May 2010.
31 *Ibid.*
32 John Gatens. "John Gatens, 589th Field Artillery Battalion, A Battery." 106th Infantry Division Association. 2006. http://www.indianamilitary. org.
33 Zaloga, *op.cit.*, 28-29.
34 Field Manual, *FM 105-mm Howitzer M2 Questions and Answers*. Field Artillery School (July 1942).

got soaked kneeling down in the puddles and mud that formed around the gun pit.

The crews on the 155mm had different challenges. Extra men were needed just to carry the shells. The 95-pound shell required bagged charges that were loaded with the shell according to the orders given by the firing officer. There were seven different propelling charges, with TNT being the most frequently used. It was the sheer weight and logistics involved with the operations of the 155mm ammo that was daunting. Shells were usually shipped in pallets, with eight shells per pallet. At the ammo dumps, these were broken down for shipment by truck to the batteries. A truck could carry between 50 and 60 shells per trip. The fuses were shipped in crates, about 25 per box. The shells had lifting rings attached at their nose during shipment, and they had to be removed to install the fuse. As with the 105mm, color markings were used to differentiate the type of shells. The setting sleeves also mirrored those on the 105mm ammo.[35] Because of the separately loaded powder, it was vital that the powder chambers of the 155mm tubes be swabbed and inspected after each round was fired. If too much powder residue built up in the barrel, it could cause a catastrophic explosion when a round was fired. Amazingly, those incidents were relatively rare considering the near constant use that most of the weapons received.

Other battery and battalion personnel included radiomen, wiremen, instrument operators (survey team), cooks, drivers, and mechanics. Many of the specialists were also grouped into sections and personnel from both the communications section and survey teams often were part of forward observation teams. Artillery batteries also had a fifth section, which was called the machine gun section. They were responsible for guarding the perimeter and hauling extra ammo.

One of the primary jobs of the instrument and survey section (also called the detail section) was to scout new positions for the battery, help lead the battery into and out of their firing positions, and lay in the guns. The skills of these men also translated into high quality artillery observers. They were also charged with conducting topographical surveys, which during combat operations were carried out rather infrequently. Upon arrival at a position, using such equipment as aiming circles, range finders, and other survey equipment like steel tapes and

[35] Timothy S. Streeter, "Ammunition for the 155mm." *Modeling the U.S. Army in World War II.* usarmymodels.com, 2002-2007, 20 October 2012. http://www.usarmymodels.com/Articles.

chains, the enlisted men of the section would lay in the guns to prepare them for aiming direction and elevation. Their officer would take a reading from the aiming circle so that the four guns of the battery would be aligned and shoot parallel with each other. The aiming circle was a small scope graduated with 6,400 mils as opposed to the usual 360 degrees (a mil is 1/6400 of a circle). It aids in laying in the guns by taking into account the Y Azimuth distance between true north and magnetic north. The reading was then given to each gunner while the howitzers were at zero deflection and a minimal elevation from level.[36]

Many of the other non-firing battery assignments came with a multitude of dangers and nowhere was that more illustrated than for the men of the wire section of HQ Battery. Their job was to lay, repair and pick up telephone line. An artillery battalion communications net was its lifeline and monitoring its operation meant constant vigilance. The risk of being spotted by enemy observers was ever present. Running a spool of black telephone cord from HQ to an observation post could put one under fire from mortars, machine guns, snipers, shelling, both friendly and German, as well as enemy patrols. The black telephone cables were constantly shot up and there were up to several miles of cable laid out between an observation post and the FDC or battery. Dense woods, thick mud and snow made repairing the lines physically demanding work. Finding the break in a line required both skill and a little bit of luck. Usually, two men were sent out. They would follow a dead line some distance, usually to a place that had just been shelled. From there, they would splice into the line with their own EE8A telephone, and crank it to ring back to their starting place. If they received an answer, they had to keep moving and the procedure was repeated until they did not get an answer. This indicated that the break was somewhere between where they were and the location of the last "Okay" call.[37]

The officers' jobs within the battery varied. Despite the copious Army manuals and regulations that defined nearly every aspect of life, the Army still encouraged low-level decision making regarding daily operations of its combat units. Junior commanders were expected to

---

[36] Baldridge, *op.cit.*, 88-89; John M. "Jack" Roberts, *Escape! The True Story of a World War II POW the Germans Couldn't Hold* (Binghamton: Brundage, 2003), 49-51; and Edward V. Walsh, *Servicing the Pieces: The 242nd Field Artillery Battalion in WWII* (West Conhohocken: Infinity Publishing, 2008), 57-59.
[37] Baldridge, *op.cit.*, 77-78.

use their own initiative. Although this concept was much more limited in the artillery branch than in other branches, in practice each battery's CO had great autonomy on officer assignments. In many cases, the executive officer ran day-to-day operations and oversaw all firing sequences and missions. Just like the enlisted, the cross training of commissioned personnel was an essential element in every battalion. The other officers could be assigned to a variety of tasks, which included motor officer, daily maintenance, firing officer or forward observer.

Duty as an observer usually occurred on a rotating basis for the officers of each battery within the battalion. A lieutenant led the small team of 3 or 4 men to a forward outpost to spend up to several days manning a front line position. There was even an instance within the 106th when a battery commander was actually manning an observation outpost at the time of the initial attack during the Bulge. When the situation was more fluid, as was the case in the summer and fall of 1944, the observation team may stay with a particular infantry unit for an extended time.

The majority of the officers within the artillery branch were highly skilled. If not West Pointers, many were from military schools such as the Virginia Military Institute (VMI) or the Citadel. Others were graduates of rigorous artillery ROTC programs from around the country. The Ivy League schools supplied the artillery branch with hundreds of officers throughout the war. Many others were reserve officers with established professional careers in civilian life. Later in the war, field commissions for qualified noncoms became common.

Another key feature of American artillery during the war was the role of non-divisional artillery battalions of all calibers. These battalions were directly under the command of their respective Corps which had its own commanders and staff to coordinate all its elements. Battalions were also formed into field artillery groups of various calibers. The groups began forming in 1943. The command element of the groups was structured very similarly to that of a divisional artillery HQ with such features as fire direction center, H&H battery and service battery. A group was usually assigned from two to six battalions. One or more of the battalions of a group might be attached for direct support to an individual division. Such was the case of the 333rd which, while still part of a group, had been directly supporting numerous infantry divisions since arriving in Europe. All of these units, regardless of their group or assignment, were considered Corps artillery.[38] In a postwar study, the Army noted that the group command structure was one of the keys to success during the war because it permitted the commanders to shift artillery battalions from army to army, corps to corps or even to support individual divisions. This way the additional fire support went where it was needed quickly.[39] During the Bulge, many of these Corps units were on the move every 12 to 24 hours. The shift of several large caliber artillery units to Bastogne during the first 48 hours of the battle helped save the city from capture.

There were 238 separate field artillery battalions operating in the ETO by war's end, with 36 105mm and 71 155mm battalions. This included self-propelled units such as the 275th Armored Field Artillery, who were positioned just north of the 106th. The other calibers were the 8 inch, the 240mm, and the 4.5 inch gun. For the larger caliber units and the armored field artillery, the number of guns per battalion differed from those of the standard infantry division artillery. Armored field artillery battalions had the same command structure within their organic divisions as the infantry, but contained 18 self-propelled howitzers instead of the usual 12 for the towed variety. The 8 inch gun and 240mm howitzer battalions had a total of six guns per battalion.[40]

REALITIES OF WAR

The artillery branch had one major problem during the war: ammunition supply. For an army famous for its ingenuity, abundance of material wealth and supposed logistical genius, this was unconscionable. Yet by the fall of 1944, the dwindling stock of artillery shells had started to become a crisis. Rationing was put into effect, with the 105mm battalions limited to 20 rounds per day per gun. Still, the war dragged on in ever-increasing intensity. During a one-month period that fall, Patton's Third Army fired over 76,000 rounds of ammunition of all types. Later in November, during the Battle for Metz, Third Army fired over 130,000 rounds over just two weeks. But that pales in

---

[38]   Richard Anderson (The Dupuy Institute), "US Army in World War II: Artillery and AA Artillery." MilitaryHistoryOnline.com, 2000. 29 March 2012.   http://www.militaryhistoryonline.com/wwii/usarmy/artillery. aspx.

[39]   Dastrup, *op.cit.*, 220-221.

[40]   Anderson, *op.cit.*

comparison to the Bulge, where during one 24-hour period alone, the American artillery battalions fired nearly 80,000 rounds. [41] By the first of January 1945, ammunition stockpiles were well below the recommended War Department levels. Despite all of this, on December 16th, most of the 106th batteries had a full stockpile of shells, but there were few reserves. And the supply depots were several miles away to the west over barely passable roads.

Another major problem that the Lion artillerymen inherited from the experienced 2nd ID was their firing positions. The 2nd had been in the Ardennes for almost two months, so they had well-built positions for both infantry and artillery. Upon the arrival of the 106th, an exchange was made with the 2nd, gun for gun, man for man. In many cases, the 2nd's artillery units just took the howitzers that the 106th brought with them, leaving their own in the existing gun pits. Extricating howitzers from their well-dug-in positions was tough work, especially in bad weather, so it made sense. But being on the front line so long also bred familiarity with your enemy, and the Germans had the American batteries zeroed. Having been so recently pushed out of the Siegfried Line fortifications, they also knew where every bunker and fortified position was located. Many of the Germans being assigned to the Ardennes in the last half of 1944 were locals who had grown up in the area. These men were part of patrols that penetrated the American lines at night, even visiting family homes. They were able to report back that nothing much had changed except that a new division was manning the line. Even with all the supposed secrecy involving the change over from one unit to another, the Germans knew exactly what unit replaced the 2nd ID. German propaganda radio broadcasts actually "welcomed" the 106th to the area. [42]

All four firing battalions were east of the Our River and in close proximity to the front line. If you include the 333rd, and the numerous other Corps battalions in the vicinity, which included 8 inch batteries, that was a lot of firepower for an enemy that was practically over the next hill. This concentrated firepower was supposed to stem any German tide that may try to roll up on the fresh troops and the entrenched artillery units, buying them time to react. The consequences

[41] *Ibid.*

[42] Elliott Goldstein, "On the Job Training: An Oral History of the Battle of Parker's Crossroads and the Fate of Those who Survived The 589th Group," 106th Infantry Division Association. 1999. http://www. indianamilitary.org.

of sustained German counter battery fire didn't seem to be considered. The Battalion COs thought differently and so did General McMahon, the *DivArty*. They were not thrilled with the situation and began immediately to make contingency plans should an attack occur. The steep ravines, dirt roads and bad weather all combined to make extricating artillery units under fire very difficult, to say nothing of resupply. Evacuation routes were mapped out, and new CPs scouted, but without the approval of the Corps commander, nothing could change. Here again, overconfidence reared its ugly head. That first week on the line, Corps intelligence just scoffed at their concerns. [43]

During the winter of 1944-45, the Allies had to fight two enemies: the Germans and the weather. Regardless of what type of gun they worked on, artillery crews and every other soldier operating in the ETO in the fall and winter of 44-45 had to learn how to adapt to the extremes of temperature. Although most of the Divisions arriving in theatre that fall had conducted winter training prior to arrival, it was nowhere near the intensity of the Northern European climate. Add to that a large number of replacements who had not had the benefit of winter training prior to hitting the front line, and there was going to be a tremendous learning curve. Every soldier out in the field had to worry about trench foot. By November, it had been become epidemic in some infantry units. The 422nd Regiment, which arrived on December 6 at Le Havre, had a severe problem with trench foot after only a week. [44] Just a few hours in wet boots, and one's feet began to turn color. For many divisions that fall, getting a hot meal was impossible with many subsisting on K rations for weeks. Heating tablets were provided, but it could not match the effectiveness of a real fire or stove. Gun crews adapted quickly. Ammunition came wrapped in treated cardboard which they were able to use to light low-grade fires. Otherwise, they resorted to burning the K Ration boxes.

Operationally, excessive cold decreased the effectiveness of a barrage. Grease in the gun barrels jelled and constant vigilance was necessary. Scrubbing with gasoline or antifreeze were favored methods to keep the muck from building up, albeit while the gun was cool. Cold weather made the powder much more unstable, and when fired, dispersion increased. Deep snow drifts also made proximity fuse ammuni-

[43] Dupuy, *op.cit.*, 14-19.

[44] *Ibid.*, 16, and Michael Tolhurst, *St. Vith: US 106th Infantry Division*, (South Yorkshire and Conshohacken, PA: Leo Cooper/Combined Publishing, 1999), 48-49.

tion burst much earlier. [45]

By the time the Army figured out that their soldiers were inadequately trained to fight in cold weather, it was too late. They would learn the hard way.

VIII Corps Disposition and Units

The 106th was part of VIII Corps, commanded by Major General Troy Middleton. Its chief divisional components also consisted of the 28th and 4th infantry division, as well as the 9th Armored Division. [46] The 28th and 4th IDs were veteran units, having landed in Normandy back in June. They were ground up mercilessly in the *Hürtgen* Forest throughout the fall, and had been assigned to the Ardennes central and southern sectors for rest and refitting. The 9th AD was new to the frontline, and still awaiting significant combat. In addition, VIII Corps had 13 general support artillery units scattered throughout the Schnee Eifel formed into various groups. Eight of the thirteen battalions were placed either in the Losheim Gap or in support of the 106th all along the twenty-mile front. [47]

African-American units played a significant role within the Corps artillery structure. There were nine non-divisional *Colored* artillery battalions along with four *Negro* Group Headquarters in the ETO scattered among several army corps. Many of these were with VIII Corps or would serve sometime under its command in the coming months. Despite the Army's policy of segregation, these men were highly trained and by December 1944, they had become some of the most experienced units in the US Army. Units were shifted according to the needs of a particular battle, so those four *Negro* Group HQs, ended up controlling both white and *Negro* battalions as the situations demanded. [48]

An 8 inch gun battalion, the 578th, a *Negro* unit, was located near the 424th Infantry Regiment at Burg Reuland. Another 8-inch gun unit was stationed around Schonberg, the all-white 740th. The 333rd Field Artillery Battalion arrived in the Ardennes with the white 771st as part of the 333rd Field Artillery Group. In the early, desperate days of the

---

[45] Doubler, *op.cit.*, 223.

[46] MacDonald, *op.cit.*, 83-84.

[47] *Ibid.*, 84.

[48] Ulysses Lee, *The Employment of Negro Troops*, United States Army in World War II (Center for Military History, 1994) 644-650.

attack, the 740th's Battery A would be attached to the 578th temporarily and put under the command of the 333rd Group. Such mixing of segregated forces was just the beginning of subtle changes in the makeup of the Army, and there would be many more cases in the weeks subsequent to the Bulge. On December 19, the 333rd Field Artillery (minus C Battery and Service Battery), was released by VIII Corps Artillery, and reassigned to support the 101st Airborne at Bastogne. The 333rd Group's new configuration included the 969th Field Artillery (*Colored*), retaining the 771st along with A and B Batteries of the 333rd field artillery. [49]

The makeup of the Corps changed considerably by the end of the battle as units were shifted between armies to various trouble spots. Along with the artillery battalions mentioned above, included under Corps command were various independent engineering battalions and a mix of other support units such as Field Artillery Observation Battalions (FAOBs), which were outfits specially trained to use sound and flash (visual) techniques to locate enemy artillery. Probably the most famous of these was Battery B of the 285th FAOB, whose personnel made up the majority of victims of the Malmédy Massacre on December 17th. As elements of the unit were making their way towards the front, they drove right into tanks of Joachim Peiper's 1st SS Panzer, and the column was nearly destroyed. After being rounded up by the SS Grenadiers, they were herded to a field near a crossroads in Baugnez, just outside Malmédy. About thirty minutes later, the Germans opened fire. 84 GIs were murdered. Many that were still alive after the firing were shot in the head or beaten to death by their SS captors. A few POWs had managed to escape, running into the nearest woods. Others escaped by feigning death and waiting for the Germans to move on. These men helped to spread the story of the killings, which led to a steely resolve on the part of GIs all over the Ardennes. [50]

The Corps' units were widely dispersed in some cases, with many units tasked in non-traditional roles. Elements of the 14th Cavalry Group along with the 275th Armored Field Artillery were charged with screening part of the Losheim Gap in the north. [51] It was a five-mile area that acted as the dividing line between the 106th and 99th ID. In theory, they were supposed to work in close consultation with the 106th's units. But like many theories, this one did not survive the test

---

[49] *Ibid.*, 647-648.
[50] MacDonald, *op.cit.*, 213-223
[51] Dupuy, *op.cit*, 25-27.

of battle. Poor communication and a lack of coordination hurt their mission. The scattered disposition of the Cavalry contributed heavily to the problems that unfolded during the first week of the Bulge. Although fighting bravely, the lightly-armored force was bowled over by the might of the Panzers in the first few days, leaving the road network behind the Schnee ridge wide open. The 275th managed to withdraw almost intact, and later contributed greatly to the defense of St. Vith.[52]

---

[52] MacDonald, *op.cit.*, 330.

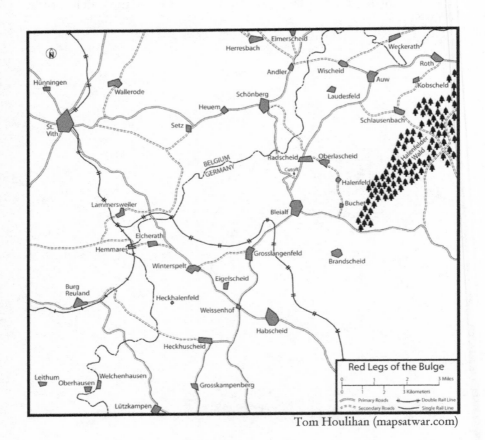

The Schnee Eifel around Schonberg

Chapter 1

Baptism of Fire

A T 0530 on Saturday, December 16, 1944, huge spotlights began bouncing off the dark clouds lighting up the darkness throughout the Ardennes region. Multicolored flares popped and hissed until finally falling to earth. Armored vehicles rumbled forward. Silent, snow-suited figures, lurking in the darkness, emerged from the woods. Even cries of *"Heil Hitler!"* were picked up by some of the startled GIs. The men at observation posts and company headquarters began trying to call their various HQs to report what was going on. Most could not get through. The lines had been cut. Radios were being jammed too. German music was about all they could pick up. A few minutes later, artillery of all calibers began flying over the front line positions. Rear areas were hit first. Buildings in St. Vith shook from the pounding. Many of the shells fell harmlessly in the woods, inflicting more damage to the nerves than the body. Some did find their mark, and many of the supporting units, especially the artillery, suffered the first wounds of the battle.

In the preceding hours between midnight and 0400 hours, these same outposts had been reporting a multitude of unusual activities on the German side. Diesel engines idled all night. Truck tailgates were slammed down with increasing frequency signaling the arrival of men and supplies. Locomotives hissed as they pulled into their stations. Animated conversations between German soldiers were clearly distinguishable. The ominous clanking and squeaking of tracked vehicles echoed everywhere in the valley. Still, repeated calls made by the nervous GIs to their various headquarters went unheeded.

THE 589TH FIELD ARTILLERY BATTALION

The 589th Field Artillery was encamped along a main road just south of the village of Auw, Germany. They had settled in the past week to provide support for the 422nd Infantry Regiment, located just to the east. The Battalion was commanded by Lieutenant Colonel Thomas Paine Kelly, a Florida attorney in civilian life. He had been uncomfortable with their positions from the day he arrived, fearing encirclement if the Germans attacked. As a result, he and his executive officer, Major Elliot Goldstein, had been drawing up plans for just such an eventuality. Within an hour of the bombardment, he sprang into action, sending his survey officer to find an area for a new CP in case the attack was larger than expected. In the meantime, his batteries readied themselves. [53]

Scottish-born John Gatens of Paterson, New Jersey, was a gunner corporal (T/5) for section one, Able Battery. One of four brothers who were all in the Army, the 19 year old was assigned to the *Golden Lions* in March of 1943. His parents emigrated from Port Glasgow to the United States when he was three, and settled in Paterson, New Jersey. John and his three brothers became typical American kids. Despite his small stature, he became a high school baseball star, playing alongside classmate and future Hall of Famer Larry Doby, who went on to become the first African-American player in the American League. After graduating from high school, he signed up with his local draft board and waited. Gatens spent the rest of 1942 and early 1943 working with his dad at the shipyards in Kearny until he was called up in February 1943. [54]

Gatens and his fellow trainload of draftees were shipped to Fort Jackson, South Carolina for their basic and division training. During the initial training period, the men were being observed by the training officers and put through a litany of tests, both physical and mental. From his group, ten men were chosen to take the test to be gunners, whose primary duty was to direct the gun on its target with information provided to him by the firing officer. John was among the only four who made it. This carried the rank of corporal. [55]

Almost two years of training made him very proficient in gun operations, and he was as confident as any solder could be upon embarking for Europe. He was eating breakfast when the onslaught began:

> I had a good plate of pancakes and strawberry jam. The shells were hitting the trees. Shell fragments and tree limbs were falling all over the place. The official thing to do under these conditions was to get back to the gun. It wasn't easy, trying not to get hit with anything that would wound or kill you. During the shelling, many rounds exploded real close and

---

[53] John Gatens. "John Gatens, 589th Field Artillery Battalion, A Battery."
[54] *Ibid.*
[55] *Ibid.*

showered dirt and tree limbs about, but also there were quite a few duds that only smacked into the ground. After about 30 minutes the shelling ceased. I did not have the foggiest notion what was going on except that we were under attack and things were becoming serious. [56]

In just a few hours, with the Germans about to overwhelm Auw, Gatens and the men of A Battery would have an encounter that most modern artillerymen could only dream about and at the same time dread: direct fire on a target.

Over at B Battery, Baltimore native John Schaffner, who was on guard duty, shared in the confusion:

> I was on guard at one of our outposts, and though I did not realize it at the time, was probably better off there than with the rest of the battery. We had a dug-in .50 Cal. MG. So, it being somewhat protected, I got down in the lowest possible place and "crawled into my helmet." Trying to get down as far as possible, I found my buttons to be in the way. We apparently did not suffer any casualties, even with all the shells that fell around the battery position. [57]

Schaffner had originally been a member of A Battery's survey section, but just prior to the Division leaving Camp Atterbury, there was a change in battery commander. The new commander's strict demeanor did not sit well with the independent-minded Schaffner. So he and his buddy Bob Stoll decided to attempt a transfer to the 82nd Airborne by going over the CO's head. Well, needless to say, that didn't go very well. John was busted to buck private and sent to B Battery. Stoll was busted too and transferred to C Battery. Despite the demotion, Schaffner was thrilled to be in a new battery. [58]

At Battalion HQ, Sergeant Randy Pierson, a fire control technician, arrived at his post that morning to see it full of concerned officers. Voices were tense. Colonel Kelly was on the phone with *DivArty*. The Battalion S-2, Captain Joe Cox, relayed plotting information to

---

[56] *Ibid.*
[57] John Schaffner. "Army Daze – A Few Memories of the Big One and Later Returns." 106th Infantry Division Association. 1995. http://www.indianamilitary.org.
[58] *Ibid.*

Major Arthur C. Parker III, the S-3 (Operations officer). Pierson had gotten a sense of the seriousness of the situation during his morning nature call. An errant shell had hit pretty close to the slit trench, sending him to the ground. With the confusion and shelling, he was happy to be in the relative safety of the CP. As a fire control technician, his job was to confirm the targeting and firing data prior to fire missions. It was a position of critical importance to the functioning of the Battalion and it gave him a ringside seat for the command decisions of the next few hours. [59]

Just after 0800 with *DivArty*'s acquiescence, Kelly made the decision to establish *CP Rear*, a new command post which would be set up along the Bleialf-Schonberg Road. As Pierson and the other noncoms began packing up to leave, Kelly called Pierson over to meet with him and Major Parker. Bluntly, Parker stated that they needed an observation post east of their HQ along the road to Prum. A series of questions followed between Kelly and Pierson about maps and strategy. Satisfied with Pierson's answers, Kelly gave him the go ahead. They needed information first and foremost, and Kelly stressed that this was not a combat mission. Like many events on this day, it would not go as planned. [60]

Once outside, Pierson quickly grabbed Privates Brown and Lemley. After their gear was packed, they headed off in an easterly direction. The group ran into the Battalion mechanic, Corporal Fairchild. He found a bazooka, and volunteered to lend a hand. Feeling more confident, the four men continued their trek.

THE 592ND FIELD ARTILLERY BATTALION

The 155mm guns of the 592nd Field Artillery Battalion were located just north and west of the 589th near the town of Laudesfeld, Germany. The Battalion was commanded by Lieutenant Colonel Richard E. Weber, a holdover from the pre-war Army. He was a West Pointer, class of 1934, and considered one of the best artilleryman in the Division. Like Kelly, he also disliked the positions astride Skyline Drive. Many felt there was no need to have another heavy unit east of the Our, especially when there were so many others in the area. In fact, there was another 155mm battalion just west of them on the Andler-

---

[59] Pierson, Randy, *op.cit.*
[60] *Ibid.*

Schonberg Road, the veteran 333rd. Roads were of poor quality and crossings over the Our River were few in number. A withdrawal under combat conditions could lead to disaster. So Weber had his staff prepare detailed plans in case of attack.

Hamilton, Ohio native Jack Roberts of C Battery, 592nd, was enjoying a good night's sleep when the attack began. He was tucked away on the second floor of an old farmhouse that housed many of the Battery's enlisted. As a scout corporal and member of the Survey Section, Roberts was scheduled to go with his forward observation team up to the front at Roth, Germany that morning; so every wink in a warm bed counted. Even after five days, many of the men were still feeling the effects of their tortuous 500 mile journey from Le Havre. He had been with the division since 1943, and was highly skilled in survey operations. At 0530, he was awakened by a thunderous barrage hitting all around him. The rumbling ground beneath him and the sound of trees being ripped apart made for a unique alarm clock. Those in the house came running out to find their lieutenants, like everyone else, not sure of what was happening. After the initial barrage lifted, things became eerily quiet again. So Roberts and his men were left with no choice but to go about their business. After a quick breakfast, they prepared to move out.[61]

The intense fog and cold did not help the mood as Roberts packed his bedroll with the others and checked on their K rations. Two vehicles, one jeep carrying Roberts, his CO Lieutenant Matson, and his driver Private Loudon, and a ¼ ton Dodge weapons carrier which held nine others moved out at around 0800 hours. In the rear of the weapons carrier was their only real defense, a pedestal-mounted .50 caliber machine gun. Also in the back of the weapons carrier, was Roberts' good friend, Howard Hoffmeyer. Before moving on to Roth, they checked in at a Division Intelligence post to find out if anything was really going on. The men were told that the shelling was normal and that they needed to proceed on with their mission.[62] The Army has always seemed to have a different definition of normal, and this day was no different.

Though the ride from Laudesfeld to Roth was only about five miles, the weather and the destruction they saw made for an ominous drive. Uprooted trees and large, black craters in the snow could be seen

---

[61]   John M. "Jack" Roberts, *Escape! The True Story of a World War II POW the Germans Couldn't Hold* (Binghamton, NY: Brundage, 2003), 109-110.
[62]   *Ibid.*, 110-111.

on both sides of the two lane road. The aroma of cordite filled the air. Although the sounds of battle had died down, their anxiety only increased. Fog made visibility difficult. They could barely see the forest that straddled the road.

About halfway to their destination, they had to pass through a clearing. With the cloud cover and fog, the party thought that they would be safe from artillery fire. No one had any idea they had just driven right into the enemy's midst. Germans were all around them. Small arms fire of all kinds ripped the air and began hitting their vehicles about halfway through the clearing. The jeep and the weapons carrier skidded to a halt. Round after round clanked against its sides. Loudon, the driver of Roberts' jeep, was hit in the shoulder, and two of the men in the weapons carrier were killed, including Roberts' buddy, Hoffmeyer. Those still left jumped out and ran for cover on either side of the road. Luck was with Roberts that day. He leapt into a ditch on the left side of the road which provided better cover. His comrades dove to the right, and were being cut down by the Germans one by one. Roberts screamed for his Lieutenant, who upon hearing his advice to move left, ran over. A couple of the others who tried to get up were mowed down. The moaning wounded and the piercing sound of tires being blown out were signals that they were done for. Despite this, Lieutenant Matson wanted to try to use the .50 cal machine gun on the weapons carrier. Roberts begged him not to try, but the obstinate Lieutenant insisted. Upon reaching the edge of the ditch, he was hit, and fell back into the hole. The two remaining unwounded men, along with Roberts, looked up to see an immense collection of armored vehicles and enemy soldiers arrayed in their direction. It was hopeless. The lieutenant gave the order, and Roberts reached in to grab a white handkerchief to tie to his carbine. [63]

The firing stopped and a horde of crazed German soldiers surged toward the stunned group. It seemed that the Krauts were either very drunk or on drugs. They were wild-eyed and mumbling. The Americans were disposed of their weapons and any personal possessions the Germans deemed valuable. Roberts lost his wristwatch, which had been a graduation present from his grandmother. As their captors continued to shout at them (they spoke no English), they motioned for Roberts and his men to move towards a cluster of trees down the

---

[63] *Ibid.*, 119-121.

RED LEGS OF THE BULGE

road. [64] After gathering themselves, and trying to aid the wounded, the men were then marched toward the Germans' forward CP. On the way, Roberts had decided against staying a prisoner. He could not stand the thought of being locked up for the rest of the war. When he would get his chance for escape, he did not know. The march continued, but this time back towards Belgium. His mind raced with worry. Where were they taking him? Will his folks be notified? The pressure was unbearable, along with the physical struggles of carrying wounded comrades. Onward they marched, through deep snow and mud. Crossing a frozen stream, Roberts and his wounded friend, Larry Loudon, fell through the ice, causing their boots to fill up with water, only adding to their misery. The Germans stood and laughed at them. [65]

To their relief, after about two miles, there was a village up ahead, which turned out to be Weckerath, Roberts' chance for escape came when just before reaching the outskirts of the village, an American light tank from one of the Cavalry units, came into view. He quickly realized an opportunity, or so he thought.

> The turret gunner on top of the tank looked down the hedge row and saw us coming. I hollered to the guys behind me, "Hit the dirt!" We all dove for the ground and that gave the turret gunner a clear view of our German guards. The Germans, not understanding English, had no idea as to what I said and just stood there. By the time the turret gunner pointed his machine gun down the lane toward the Germans for a line of fire, the tank driver, being down inside the tank and unaware of our plight, continued driving past the intersection. [66]

Thankfully, an alert American sergeant marching behind the tank toting a Thompson pursued Roberts' captors and finished them off. Upon reaching the village, they were met by a Captain from the 14th Calvary, who told them to hold off on any celebrations, for their freedom might only be temporary. They were still surrounded, and had to make a run for Manderfeld, one mile to the west. Both the Americans and Germans had the village zeroed, and signs of destruction were all around. Weapons were scarce. The troopers had no rifle for Roberts, but handed him four grenades. The Captain came up with a plan to get

---

[64] *Ibid.*, 121-123.
[65] *Ibid.*, 123-127.
[66] *Ibid.*, 128.

every one out in two waves, including the wounded. Basically, the two groups, separated by a few minutes, would just drive down the road at top speed. By some miracle, they all made it, though once again, relief was temporary.[67]

Manderfeld was about to be surrounded as well, the Cavalry could not hold and their aid station was getting full. Roberts was determined to get back to the 592nd. He borrowed a compass from one of the Cavalry officers and along with two others from the ill-fated convoy, Terrill Rigdon and Harold Hallberg, disappeared into the darkness. It was nearly 1800 hours. There was no moon. The sky was overcast. Without a map or watch, keeping time and direction was almost impossible. In order to get out, they would have to follow the Germans towards the frontline, bypass their enemy, and infiltrate through American lines, all while trying to convince nervous GIs that they were not the enemy.[68]

THE 590TH FIELD ARTILLERY BATTALION

Headquartered in the German village of Radscheid, just off *Skyline Drive*, the 590th FAB was assigned to support the 423rd Infantry Regiment, which lay south and west of them. The batteries were relatively spread out, with A Battery down the road in Oberlascheid, B Battery near the Radscheid HQ and C Battery slightly to the northwest of the village. Leading the Battalion was a 43-year old Princeton-educated attorney from Tennessee, Lieutenant Colonel Vaden Lackey. Besides his age (he had just celebrated his birthday on the 14th), the touches of gray around his temples gave revelation to his moniker as the *Old Man*.

At his machine gun outpost just outside of the village of Oberlascheid, Able Battery Sergeant Pete House of Jacksonville, Florida sat spellbound when the kaleidoscope of spotlights and flares started. As the shells began to fall, he and his two buddies felt the tenuousness of their position growing exponentially and knew something big was going on. They were an island in the middle of nowhere, their only lifeline the thick, black telephone cord connecting them back to the battery. Of course, this was quickly cut. The other men at the batteries began to stir, and confusion spread immediately. Most of the officers responded quickly, getting the men on their guns, while others fin-

---

[67] *Ibid.*, 128-132.
[68] *Ibid.*, 133-134.

RED LEGS OF THE BULGE

ished up a quick breakfast before heading to their assigned tasks. Everyone was awaiting orders from Battalion HQ.

Sergeant (T/4) Richard Ferguson, of the 590th's Headquarters battery, had been *volunteered* for observer duty by Colonel Lackey. He told Ferguson that it would be a trial period in preparation for a field commission. His timing could not have been worse, for he assumed his post on the evening of December 15:

> The first night we spent in the pill box we were hit repeatedly with the multiple rockets called screaming meemies. The sound was deafening inside the pillbox. The next morning I could see all kinds of movement in our direction. There were wagons with tree branches lashed to the sides filled with soldiers. There were many on bicycles and many on foot. I tried to communicate with our gun batteries but could not get through by radio or phone. When I left the pill box, I could not recognize the area at all. Trees were down all over. Our telephone wires were mangled in the trees. [69]

Ferguson managed to get back to the HQ, and needed no convincing that this was a serious attack. In some ways, he was surprised to be here. Prior to the war, he had worked at a plant making airplane parts, and that earned him a draft deferment once the war began. By 1943, new manufacturing designs made his position obsolete, and his deferment was gone. So off he went to the Army. With his skills, he earned his stripes fairly quickly, which got him a posting to Headquarters Battery. [70]

Battalion Survey Sergeant Richard Hartman was at Battalion HQ when the barrage started. Shortly afterward, *DivArty* ordered the Battalion to alternate positions over the Our. So Hartman and his survey section headed out toward Schonberg to seek out the new positions. As they drove down the hill into the village, a massive bombardment began to rain down. It continued as they sped through the village and on towards St. Vith. They were finally forced to seek cover off the road. Their survey officer and his driver decided to head to St. Vith for orders. After three hours of futility, they were finally ordered back to

---

[69] Richard Ferguson. "Sgt. T/4 Richard C. Ferguson 31329406," 106th Infantry Division Association. 2006. http://www.indianamilitary. org.

[70] Richard Ferguson, Letter to Author, December 26, 2010.

Battalion HQ.[71]

THE 591ST FIELD ARTILLERY BATTALION

Located on the Division's southern flank, the gun positions of the 591st FAB started receiving intermittent artillery fire as early as 2400 hours on the 15th, along with a smattering of small arms fire. No one thought it more than the usual harassment by the enemy. As dawn approached, the firing got heavier, and their feelings began to change.[72]

The unit was commanded by Lt. Colonel Phillip Hoover. The energetic Oklahoman had been in the National Guard at the outbreak of the war before becoming a gunnery instructor at Fort Sill, and then finally the commander of the 591st when it was activated in 1943. All that time training his men paid off in the early hours of the battle. As the heavy bombardment rained down around 0530, his cannoneers responded with great force while under tremendous pressure. Pouring round after round in support of the 424th, the Germans were repulsed several times during the day. Enemy bodies were described as "piling up" in front of the infantry's outposts. There was no doubt in their minds that this attack was more than a reconnaissance in force. The Battalion's ability to holdout was in serious question by midday. Hoover held meetings throughout the day with his staff and that of Regimental. He communicated his opinions to the Division Artillery. A plan was needed immediately, he stressed, to extricate both the 424th and the 591st.[73]

The batteries were in difficult positions. Two batteries, A and B, were well forward in sugar bowl-like positions. C Battery was the furthest south. Their infantry protection was thin due to their extra responsibility of not only holding the line on the Germans, but making sure they tied in with the 28th Division on their right flank.[74] The 424th was responsible for covering more than six miles of front, the largest of any of the regiments, an area normally covered by an entire division.

---

[71] Richard Hartman, "590th Field Artillery Battalion," 106th Infantry Division Association. http://www.indianamlitary.org. This was a reprint of an article first appearing in the Association's newsletter, *The Cub*, April-May 1949 edition, vol. 5, no. 5.

[72] Robert Ringer, "My Adventures in Europe in World War II." 106th Infantry Division Association. 2006. http://www.indianamilitary.org.

[73] *Ibid.*

[74] Dupuy, *op.cit.*, 52-53.

Because of this unusual layout and the rough terrain, extrication would be a harrowing experience: leapfrogging each other, bypassing the enemy and in some cases, driving right through them, before they could make it to the Our River.

Lieutenant Robert Ringer, Service Battery's ammunition officer, had spent the first week in the Ardennes trying to get to know the area despite a lack of adequate maps. A 1942 graduate of Ohio State University, he received his commission through its ROTC program the same year and was subsequently inducted into the Regular Army as a second lieutenant. His first two years were spent in various duties, including an ROTC instructor at his alma mater until finally being assigned to the 591st in January 1944.[75]

After an all-night drive from Verviers for ammunition, Lieutenant Ringer was in a deep sleep when his Sergeant gave him a tap in the back with his carbine. An angry Ringer was telling his noncom where to put his weapon when the Sergeant politely suggested that he come see "the light show." Intrigued, Ringer ran out and knew right away there was trouble. Artillery *crumped* in the distance, and there was a smattering of small arms fire echoing in the valley. But despite the unease, he initially went about his job like it was just another day, first hauling coal to the Battalion, then checking on ammunition.[76]

But Ringer's eventful day was just beginning. He would be ambushed at Winterspelt, shot in the boot, manage to pick up another supply of ammunition, fall asleep on the way back (and so did the driver), pull the supply column over for a drink of scotch and still get back to Burg Reuland safely. It was to become a typical day for men fighting in the Bulge, except for the supply of Scotch.[77]

Throughout the day, he was reminded of an incident that had occurred the previous Tuesday while on an ammunition run. As was the case throughout Europe, the young children of the liberated towns and villages gravitated towards the generous GIs. Communication was always a problem due to language differences, but this time was different. One of Ringer's men, Sergeant Karl Drysrmala, spoke excellent German, so one of the local boys struck up a conversation with him. To their astonishment, the boy related that his dad was a German soldier who frequently visited home by bypassing the American outposts. The information was immediately sent to their Battalion S-2, who sent

---

[75] Ringer, *op.cit.*
[76] *Ibid.*
[77] *Ibid.*

it straight to Division. The perimeter guards were doubled, but nothing else came of the incident, except for some nervous sentries firing into the dark.[78]

Like the other Battalions, the 591st's situation worsened as the 16th became the 17th. The Battalion expended 2,622 shells the first day, virtually their entire supply.[79] Seven truckloads of shells and powder charges lay waiting in St. Vith. To avoid encirclement, would take skill, luck and a lot of daring.

THE 333RD FIELD ARTILLERY BATTALION

The 333rd Field Artillery Battalion (155mm), like most African-American artillery battalions, was a non-divisional unit under the command of its Army Corps, in this case, VIII Corps. Its Group, also called the 333rd, had, at various times, both white and black units. Situated along the Andler-Schonberg Road, the Battalion had been in position since early October. After the departure of the 2nd Division, it was nominally attached to the 106th as supplemental fire support. Two observation teams were posted in and around the German village of Bleialf. A liaison officer, Captain John P. Horn, had been posted with the 590th Field Artillery.[80]

The Battalion had something many of their neighboring units did not have: combat experience. Commanded by Lieutenant Colonel Harmon Kelsey, a white officer, the Battalion had been in the field since late June '44, when it landed at Utah Beach. It fired its first shots just hours after arriving. Eventually, it ended up supporting the 2nd Infantry Division as it moved into the Ardennes in the early fall. Its main gun was the standard towed M114 155mm howitzer, and it had the standard table of organization, very similar to the 592nd. Despite the segregation of the era, some of its junior officers were black. The Battalion had an impressive record, once firing 1500 rounds in a 24 hour period and actually capturing a village in France. And for once, a black unit received some recognition. Yank Magazine ran an article

---

[78] *Ibid.*

[79] Dupuy, *op.cit.*, 59.

[80] Raymond E. Bell, Jr., "Black Gunners at Bastogne." *Army*, Nov. 2004. elibrary (King County Library System, King County, WA). October 9, 2012. http://elibrary.bigchalk.com.ezproxy.kcls.org/elibweb.

devoted entirely to the Battalion in the fall of 1944.[81]

The Corps artillery units which had been in the vicinity for some time, such as the 578th and the 740th, along with the 333rd, had built up their positions so well that almost every GI was billeted in a log cabin, house, or well-insulated tent. The black 578th, down at Burg Reuland with a battalion of the 424th, had a bowling alley built and regular visits from the Red Cross Clubmobiles. Regular leave was instituted to either Paris or other cities in Belgium. For African-American soldiers in a segregated army, morale was high and conditions mirrored that of their white counterparts.[82]

On the 16th, with the scope of the Battle still unknown, Corps ordered A and B Battery to displace west of the river with the rest of their group, eventually moving south into Bastogne. C Battery along with Service Battery and the Battalion HQ staff were to remain in place for now at the request of General McMahon of the 106th. He believed their fire support would be needed in case of a withdrawal. With shells flying over the river, and some falling just in front of their positions, it began receiving calls from its observers in Bleialf for support, which they were able to provide almost immediately. C Battery, commanded by Captain George MacCloud, was to play a large part in the defense of the Schnee Eifel this first day of the battle, helping to deny the Germans a permanent foothold in Bleialf on the 16th.

MacCloud, an Oklahoma native, had one of the toughest jobs an officer could have in a segregated Army. He was a white officer in command of black troops. Not only did he need to relate to his men, whose life experiences were polar opposites of his own, but he had to earn the respect of other white officers who often looked down on those in his position. MacCloud certainly had the respect of his men. Newark, New Jersey native Sergeant George Schomo, called MacCloud a great commander, a man's man and someone he would have followed anywhere.[83]

There was no immediate concern about encirclement. Being fairly close to the river and its heavy, stone bridges would enable them to get out quickly if needed. After all, they assumed, with its other batteries already on the move, it would be only a matter of time before the or-

---

[81] "Negro Artillery in World War II," *Field Artillery Journal*, Vol. 36, No. 4, April 1946: 228-229.

[82] Lee, *op.cit.*, 646.

[83] Jean Paul Pallud, "Putting a Name to a Face," *After the Battle*, No. 144. 2009: 50-55.

ders came down to get on the road.

Other Corps artillery units were given march orders within hours, although in some cases, they first had to stand and fight. The men of the 578th, whose batteries were well forward, had to pick up M-1 Garands and fight as infantry to hold off the onslaught, taking 12 prisoners.[84] Despite the stern defense, by nightfall these units had to continue their preparations to displace, only to be held up by the growing traffic jam.

THE END OF THE BEGINNING

Things deteriorated quickly by late morning. German panzers and infantry were pouring through the Losheim Gap to the north, Bleialf was about to be overrun, and the southern flank of the 424th was barely holding.

By noon, Auw had been seized and the German force surged toward Andler. With Teutonic efficiency, they also sent a small force of self-propelled guns, called *Sturmgeschütze (StuG IIIs)*, down the Auw-Bleialf road, immediately threatening the 589th. Around 1400 hours, the three guns swept past the outposts of Headquarters battery and then headed down towards A Battery.[85] Once past the 589th, the force could then cut off the 590th along with the remaining infantry units, and essentially seal off access to the Auw road. Waiting nervously beside the road, John Gatens and his crew began tracking the lead *StuGIII* as it came into view. All of his training now had to come to the fore. Squinting into his telescopic sight, Gatens tried to get a bead on the armored behemoth as it ponderously came toward A Battery. Two of the battery's officers were perched above the road trying to call down accurate fire.

To the Americans' surprise, they held a slight advantage. The road was slightly elevated for grading. The gun crew was located on the left side of the road, and at a slightly lower angle, they were in a perfect position to inflict serious damage to the Panzer. Unlike a Sherman's 75mm gun, which had a very difficult time against German tanks, the 105mm howitzer, with a much more powerful shell, could penetrate most German frontal armor. American tanks were forced to hit the tracks or get behind the panzers in order to hit them in the engine

---

[84] Lee, *op.cit.*, 647.
[85] Dupuy, *op.cit.*, 40-41.

RED LEGS OF THE BULGE

compartment.

With chaos the order of the day, nothing was going to be easy. Interrupting Gatens' concentration, four GIs came running down the hill between the *StuGIII* and his 105mm. Gatens jumped from behind his scope, bravely ran in front of the gun, and began waving like mad to get their attention. Finally seeing the corporal, the men hit the ground. Gatens then got back behind the plate and began tracking once again. He shook from the adrenalin coursing through his body. The first shot missed. His crew immediately reloaded and fired again. It was a hit. Flames burst everywhere. The crew began bailing out, only to be cut down by small arms fire. Two more *StuGIIIs* got hit behind the first one but were able to withdraw without further damage. Gatens and his men took a deep breath but knew more was to come. [86]

Oblivious to the action swirling west of them, Randy Pierson and his makeshift squad had situated themselves astride one of the main east-west roads that lead down from the Schnee ridge. Pierson spread the men out. Lemley was sent 100 yards east. Brown was sent to the top of the hill to act as radioman. Pierson and Fairchild remained on the south slope of the hills. They quietly sat in whiteout-like conditions with the temperature hovering in the teens, hoping and praying that the enemy was not heading their way. [87]

Their hopes were quickly dashed as the faint sounds of tank treads grew louder. Pierson told Brown to call Battalion HQ immediately. Disregarding the order to not initiate any contact, Pierson and Fairchild assembled the bazooka and readied it to fire. They watched warily as out of the fog below them as a Panther emerged, its commander sticking out of the hatch. Fairchild tapped Pierson on the shoulder to indicate the bazooka was ready to go. He let loose a shot that hit the side of the tank just above its tracks. The shot inflicted very little damage despite the deafening noise and thick smoke. They reloaded and tried again. This time it hit the drive sprocket and disabled the lead tank. The road was now blocked but the Panther could still shoot and it did. [88] The 75mm cannon sent a blast right towards the men:

> The powerful muzzle blast at close range, plus the savage concussion caused by the passing high velocity projectile, tore

---

[86] Gatens, "John Gatens, 589th Field Artillery Battalion."
[87] Randy Pierson, *op.cit.*
[88] *Ibid.*

away my helmet and knocked me flat. In the process, the chin strap of the helmet scratched my face and severely tore my nose, causing blood to flow freely. As I lay on the ground dazed, unable to move, my ears ringing, my sight blurred, and my life's blood staining the white snow red, I thought, "God, is this where I am going to die?" [89]

Pierson eventually passed out. He regained consciousness, and found his buddies. With artillery and small arms fire crackling all around them, they left the hill and began the long march back to the Battalion. Six hours later, they reached A Battery's perimeter.

As the 589th was facing down the Germans, the men of the 590th were dealt a severe blow. The entire Battalion had been intermittently shelled all morning. But a heavier barrage rained down on Oberlascheid just before midday blasting away at A Battery's positions. Men were sent scrambling. Unfortunately, not all made it to cover. Captain John Pitts, the 26 year-old commander of A Battery, was caught out in the open near the mess hall when a shell exploded nearby. A piece of shrapnel hit him just underneath his helmet, killing him instantly. [90] The stunned artillerymen went about the grim task of rounding up their casualties, and the Battery's executive officer, Lieutenant Rex Rhoden, had the unenviable task of becoming battery commander. He immediately reassessed the situation and called Major Meadows, the Battalion Executive. All the Major could do was offer a sympathetic ear and try to comfort the now overburdened new CO. Rhoden, like all of the COs, had one worry, ammunition. Although the batteries had gotten their full allotment before the attack, by nightfall, many of the batteries were at half strength. A Battery's stockpile was nearly depleted. Many of the stockpiles still sat at supply depots on the other side of the Our. [91]

The death of Captain Pitts, a 1941 University of Illinois grad, was especially poignant because his twin sister was just a few miles away, working as a Red Cross volunteer. She had visited with her brother earlier in the week and was excited that their *Clubmobile* would be entering the zone of the 106th for an extended stay. She received news of

---

[89] *Ibid.*

[90] Pete House. "My Experiences During the Battle of the Bulge," 106th Division Association, 2006, http://www.indianamilitary.org; and E.V. Creel, phone interview with Author, October 2005.

[91] E.V. Creel, Phone interview, 8 October 2005.

his death upon arrival in St. Vith. Division headquarters staff quickly sent Ms. Pitts and her fellow volunteers back to the rear. In another coincidence, just after leaving Camp Standish, Massachusetts for their embarkation in Boston, Pitts saw his brother, who was also in Boston preparing for deployment. The Captain was excited about going over-seas. His first couple of years in the Army had been as an instructor at Fort Bragg, but it was frustrating. He had wanted to get in the fight. Like so many men who volunteered, he paid the ultimate price for his bravery.[92]

As word spread of the fall of Auw and the imminent threat to Andler, the idea of withdrawal became the foremost thought for all the commanders. By late afternoon, it was obvious what the Germans were trying to do. Manteuffel's forces sought to envelop the 106th on the Schnee Eifel and make a dash for St. Vith. Whenever communications allowed, the battalion and regimental commanders rang up Division HQ to let them know what was happening. Division realized the threat, but was unable to put together a clear plan of either counterattack or defense because all of the Division's resources were already committed. The only reserve remaining, the 423rd's 2nd battalion which had been billeted up near St. Vith, was being alerted to move out and head for Schonberg.[93] The tiny village was now center stage, and the fate of thousands of GIs hinged on holding it open. No serious thought appears to have been given to blowing the bridge in case the Germans got too close. Earlier, the 1st Battalion, 424th Infantry, the other reserve unit, had been released to Colonel Reid. General Jones was left to rely on promises of help from both the 7th and 9th Armored Divisions. He needed time. Most of Division HQ's responses involved placating the COs to allay fears of encirclement. Luckily for many in the 106th, the gumption and determination of their own small unit commanders ruled the day. They had been scoffed at by Corps before the attack, but now they were going to take matters into their own hands.

Portions of Bleialf fell temporarily that day to the 295th Regiment of the 18th Volksgrenadier Division. Throughout the morning, the 106th's Cannon Company and various antitank units held out long enough around the fringes of Bleialf to allow Colonel Cavender of the 423rd Infantry Regiment to gather forces for a counterattack later in the

---

[92] Richard Hartman, "590th Field Artillery Battalion," 106th Infantry Division Association, http//:www.indianamlitary.org. This was a reprint of an article first appearing in *The Cub*, April-May 1949 edition, vol. 5, no. 5.
[93] Dupuy, *op.cit.*, 42-43.

day. With help from the 423rd's Service Company, they retook much of the village. Even with enemy reinforcements pouring up the road from Sellerich, the Americans managed to keep a toehold in the village throughout the night and dealt a severe blow to the Germans' timetable.[94] Despite their bravery, American losses continued to mount. Among the first day's casualties was Captain James Manning, Cannon Company CO. Manning, a Citadel graduate, was killed by enemy fire during close quarter fighting in the village's dairy just hours after the initial assault.[95]

Numerous American personnel trapped in isolated pockets around the village kept up the fight. Battery A of the 16th Field Artillery Observation Battalion, a Corp unit, had an outpost near the railroad tunnel until they were finally overrun with several personnel managing to escape.[96] A five-man observer team from Baker Battery, 590th, called in numerous fire missions throughout the day and night. Lts. Zane Donaldson and Charles N. Schenck, III, radio operators T/4 Eugene Womack and T/5 Akey, and driver Pfc, Donald Sheehy, directed fire throughout the day. Having been forced out once already, they returned to Bleialf with the infantry and continued to observe for the Battalion. Donaldson, Womack and Sheehy remained in Bleialf till the next day. Miraculously, all escaped. Womack got out on foot while Donaldson and Sheehy drove a jeep right through German lines. The jeep had two punctured tires and was riddled with holes. All three were recommended for the Silver Star. Schenck and Akey were recommended for the Bronze Star.[97]

Two forward observer groups from the 333rd FAB also had their outposts on the edge of the village and held their ground. One was led by Lieutenant Reginald Gibson, and the other by Lieutenant Elmer King. Whenever communication allowed, they kept identifying targets for any artillery battery that would listen. Both groups managed to stay at their posts until 0600 the next day. It was a remarkable achievement considering they were almost completely surrounded by

---

[94] *Ibid.*, 46-52.
[95] *Ibid.*, 50.
[96] Captain Charles M. Hunter, "History of the 16th FAOB and our experiences in the Battle of the Bulge." Center for Research and Information on the Battle of the Bulge, 11 December 2008, 1 Oct. 2012 http//:www.criba.be.
[97] Hartman, *op.cit.*

RED LEGS OF THE BULGE

the enemy for nearly 24 hours. [98]

Any seeming advantage that the Americans had was being nullified this day. Airpower was grounded. Resupply was becoming a pipe dream. The communications net proved to be the most fragile. Radio transmission was spotty at best. Much of that was due to the weather. Wire crews were stretched thin trying to find breaks in the line. Runners between the regiments and the artillery battalions spread out across the Eifel trying to get messages between units. Even when the system was working, it was taking hours to get a message through. The Division switchboard was overwhelmed. These delays caused mass confusion and had grave consequences. Poor planning was the culprit. The Division switching station was located in the now threatened village of Schonberg. Like so many other things, they had inherited both the station and the communications network set up from the 2nd ID. And there was one serious design flaw. Although each of the Division's infantry regiments had two lines going to and from, both were laid within one large cable. So if that cable was cut, all communication would be lost. The same was true for the links between the regiments and their artillery battalions. [99]

Uncertainty reigned by evening. The 590th was still in position. The 589th and 592nd were preparing for withdrawal. The 591st was still considering the best way to get out while still covering the 424th's withdrawal. Its A and B Batteries were still holding firm in their *sugar bowl* positions which had became a salient in the Germans' drive; but only one small road was left open as an avenue of escape. Roads were beginning to get choked with traffic, much of it from Corps units that had received orders to reposition west of the Our.

The tide was rising on the 106th, and their commanders' decisions in the next few hours would decide their fate.

---

[98] Bell, *op.cit.*
[99] Dupuy, *op.cit.*, 60-61.

John Gatens

Corporal John Gatens

John Schaffner

Corporal John Schaffner

RED LEGS OF THE BULGE

Carl Wouters

Eric Wood at Princeton

John Schaffner

John Schaffner during observer training

RED LEGS OF THE BULGE

John Schaffner

Men of the 589th prepping shells at Fort Jackson, South Carolina, 1943.

Carl Wouters

Battery A, 589th at Camp Atterbury, summer 1944

RED LEGS OF THE BULGE

Jack Roberts

Sgt. Jack Roberts in early 1945.

Carl Wouters

Major Arthur C. Parker III

Carl Wouters

Lt. Albert Martin

Carl Wouters

Lt. Col. Thomas Paine Kelly

Carl Wouters

Lt. Col. Vaden Lackey

Carl Wouters

Village of Schonberg in a pre-war photo.

Carl Wouters

Gun section of the 591st.

Carl Wouters

105mm crew packing the shells.

RED LEGS OF THE BULGE

NARA

A 155mm howitzer crew from the 333rd at Normandy.

Captain MacCloud and some of his men.

Traffic outside St. Vith on December 16, 1944.

Roberts/Bundesarchiv

The body of Howard Hoffmeyer. His boots were stolen.

RED LEGS OF THE BULGE

Jack Roberts

The locations of Jack Roberts' ambush photographed in the 1990s.

Carl Wouters

The last known photo of Lt. Wood, taken December 14, 1944.

RED LEGS OF THE BULGE

The Wereth 11. Photo taken by Army Signal Corps just after bodies were found.

NARA

Lt. Ivan Long and his men at St. Vith after their escape.

NARA

Baraque de Fraiture in a postwar photo.

Claude Orban

John Gatens and John Schaffner (center) visiting Eric Wood's grave.

Claude Orban

John Schaffner and John Gatens during a ceremony at Parker's Crossroads in 2012.

NARA

A forward observer team in early 1945.

A cannon company wireman during the Bulge.

NARA

A standard fire direction center in 1944.

RED LEGS OF THE BULGE

NARA

Crew of a 105mm howitzer in 1944.

NARA

Crew of a 155mm howitzer in action, fall 1944.

Ammo man prepping 155mm shells.

NARA

#1 gunner (right side of breach) adjusting elevation on a 105mm.

An 8-inch howitzer during the Bulge.

NARA

A 240mm howitzer in Italy 1944.

M7 Howitzer Motor Carriage (105mm).

NARA

The howitzers of the 590th Field Artillery still in their positions in February 1945.

NARA

M12 Gun Motor Carriage (155mm) being cleaned.

NARA

Slow going in the Bulge: Tanker truck stuck in the snow.

NARA

A line of L-4 observation aircraft awaiting orders.

John Schaffner

May 1945: A happy John Schaffner celebrates the end of the War in Europe.

RED LEGS OF THE BULGE

Chapter 2

17 December
The Ring Tightens

AS another cold, gray dawn broke on Sunday the 17th, there was a general feeling throughout the entire division that this would be a decisive day. By now the scope of the attack was becoming clearer, and a decision had to be made regarding a full withdrawal and the use of their remaining reserves. The GIs had maintained a tenuous hold on Bleialf, but by early morning it was obvious that another large scale German attack was imminent. To the north, the Germans were seen moving on Andler. The perimeters around the 422nd and 423rd infantry regiments were being pressured by German patrols that probed for weak spots. The artillery battalions were preparing to move out (*March Order* in artillery parlance). The Americans were desperately trying to maintain control over the Auw road. Access to the Our River bridges could be lost if the Germans attacked in force within the next few hours.

The 592nd had gotten out first. Late on the 16th, Col. Weber heard from *DivArty*, that they needed to withdraw over the river as soon as possible. Hauling guns that each weighed over 12,000 pounds was not easy. But Weber had his men ready to go. In the wee hours of the morning, they got through Schonberg and set up gun positions as soon as they could. The escape was not without losses, however. While moving from their positions near Laudesfeld, one section of A Battery along with members of Service Battery turned left at the Bleialf-Schonberg Road junction when they should have turned right. Heading into Bleialf, they were ambushed by German patrols and cut off. Most were killed or captured. A few survivors managed to get back to the 590th HQ where their story provided a cautionary tale for their fellow *Lions*.[100] By mid-morning, the Battalion was safely ensconced west of the Our, though not for long. The pressure on St. Vith was

---

[100] Lt. Col. Richard Weber Jr., Commander, 592nd Field Artillery Battalion. December 10-31, 1944 After Action Report. 106th Infantry Division Association. http://www.indianamilitary.org.

about to grow immensely, and they would have to turn their support toward the defense of that beleaguered city.

The 591st continued pouring fire down on the enemy advancing toward the 424th. In the most forward areas near Heckhalenfeld, A and B batteries' positions remained under enormous pressure. They were practically surrounded. Snipers came close enough to harass the cannoneers. The men manning the guns would drop down while the snipers' bullets pinged against the guns' steel frame. As soon as the Germans were chased away, they would bravely jump back on their guns to fire another mission. Escape routes from the salient were few, and ammo runs were becoming suicide missions. Not everyone was sticking around. While on an ammo run that morning, Ringer witnessed a neighboring Corps Artillery unit hastily pulling out along with the MPs, who were hot on their heels. Within a matter of hours there might be nothing behind the battalion except Germans.[101]

The line between strategic withdrawal and rout was getting thinner. Despite the presence of a small force from the 9th Armored, the situation only worsened. Combat-weary stragglers from the 424th and 28th Division were emerging from the woods. Survivors from the 28th (112th IR) had reported being overrun. Their entire regiment was in full retreat. This meant the Division's southern flank was now wide open. Reid and Hoover carefully formulated several less than appealing scenarios to get their men out while anxiously waiting on word from Division.

The 590th was packing up and believed it was heading over the Our later in the day with Lieutenant Colonel Joseph Puett's 2nd Battalion (423rd) guarding its rear. Puett's unit had been in Division reserve north of St. Vith until finally released into the fight late on the 16th. After spending the night in Schonberg, they were ordered to cover the Auw road as the artillery displaced down this critical north-south route.[102] The 590th fired its last mission from its original positions at 0630 in response to a frantic call from the 423rd.[103]

But first, it was the turn of the 589th. For all the struggles and successes they had had on the 16th, that day would pale in comparison to the events in and around Schonberg this critical morning. Avoiding capture or death became the primary goal. One story of escape became legendary, and it remains controversial to this day.

---

[101] Ringer, *op.cit.*

[102] Dupuy, *op.cit.*, 84-85

[103] *Ibid.*, 89.

At 0400, the Battalion moved out to emplace near their Service Battery which was stationed just south Schonberg, astride the road leading to Bleialf. Almost all of A and B Batteries had gotten out, but C Battery remained mired in the muck. Its howitzers were unable to be budged. With enemy patrols closing in fast, Colonel Kelly volunteered to stay and help the Battery get their guns out. Majors Goldstein and Parker would lead the way to the new emplacements. [104]

It was a rough ride particularly over the corduroy road that had been built by the Engineers known as the *Cutoff*. It was built to avoid the aptly named *Purple Heart Corner*. The corner was a sharp turn at the junction where the Auw road connects to the Schonberg-Bleialf road. The Germans had the intersection zeroed from their perch in Brandscheid. Anyone who ventured to the corner in daylight would come under fire, so a road had been constructed through the forest by the 2nd Division Engineers earlier that fall and the 106th's own 81st Engineers improved it upon arrival. [105] It was essentially a dirt path about 500 yards long in which the engineers had embedded railroad ties and logs. By December, the road proved to be no safe haven. John Gatens remembers the harrowing trip:

> The big trucks churned the icy muck into a paste in which the guns sank almost hub deep. Hostile small arms and artillery fire were sweeping the area. Snow blew into sweating faces in the night. The wind howled through the trees, each of which might be hiding an infiltrating enemy soldier. All of the gun crews had to help all the guns and trucks pull and push until we had cleared the corduroy road. [106]

Upon reaching their new home, three guns of A Battery were emplaced along the road. One gun crew which had gotten into a fender bender was a late arrival and put up as anti-tank defense down the road. B Battery soon followed suit. So the two batteries along with Service Battery began going about their business as best they could, readying themselves for another mission or an order to withdraw. They wouldn't have to wait long. At 0715 hours, Service Battery rang the new Battalion HQ. Enemy tanks and infantry were coming up the road. While speaking, the line went out. Minutes later, one of their

---

[104] Col. Thomas P. Kelly, The Fighting 589th (1stBooks, 2001), 78-85.
[105] Dupuy, *op.cit.*, 131.
[106] Gatens, "John Gatens, 589th Field Artillery Battalion, A Battery."

trucks came barreling up the road to the new HQ. Word was passed once again to the batteries, "March Order." There would be no time for an organized withdrawal. In minutes, the Germans were within 100 yards of B Battery's position, so their howitzers had to be disabled and abandoned. Under heavy enemy fire, Schaffner, along with his crew from HQ Battery, jumped into any vehicles they could find and hit the road before the main group. They managed to get through Schonberg just minutes ahead of the Germans. [107]

Three sections of Battery A, which included Gatens and his crew, quickly packed up and escaped through Schonberg. They also picked up the last remaining operators at the switching station. They headed immediately for St. Vith. Fate stepped in the way again for the last section. While making its way to the road, one of the trucks pulling the gun got stuck. Section chief, Sgt. Scannapico and his men, along with Lieutenant Eric Wood, the battery executive, stayed behind to help get it loose. Wood was now acting CO due to Captain Aloysius Menke posting himself up at one of the observation posts the night of the 15th. No one had heard from him since. After some time, they freed the gun. With most of B Battery trailing, they made their way down into the village.

The spire of the Church of Saint George could be seen towering over the village and beyond that lay the stone bridge. Smoke was still billowing from some of the chimneys; maybe there was a chance of getting through unscathed. Escape was tantalizingly close. But as they came down the hill, seven members of the 333rd Field Artillery were rushing up towards them, waving frantically. They had been overrun from their positions near Andler. Reaching Schonberg, they found the Germans already there and were now trying to warn their fellow GIs that the way was blocked. Disregarding their warnings, the convoy pressed on, and ready to run a gauntlet of enemy fire if necessary. Upon crossing the Our river bridge, they were met by German armor and infantry. Scannapico rushed from his truck with a bazooka and was riddled by machine gun fire, which killed him instantly. A panzer opened fire on the truck and killed the driver, Ken Knoll. Lt. Wood and his men leapt from their vehicles and ran for cover. The trucks from B Battery began pulling up behind them. German infantry was picking them off one by one. With no chance to fight back, most of

---

[107] Schaffner, *op.cit.*

the men began putting their hands up in surrender. [108]

As the men were herded from the ditches, shots began ringing out again. Guttural shouts in German echoed everywhere. The men carefully peered up to see Wood making a run for the tree line just outside of town. Rounds tore up the dirt between his legs. The husky lieutenant kept going and going until he disappeared into a labyrinth of fir and pine. It was the last time any of his men would see him alive. His body, with that of another unidentified GI, was found in early February 1945 just over 10 miles northwest of Schonberg near the village of Meyerode. After the area was retaken by the Americans, local villagers led the GIs to the bodies. Surrounding Wood and his comrade were the bodies of numerous German soldiers. All of Wood's personal effects including his wallet containing Belgian Francs were still on his body. This indicated he was probably the last to die because the Germans would have certainly taken the money or anything else of value. [109]

What we know about the events in between December 17, 1944 and the following February was gleaned from an Army investigation and Wood's father's review of what occurred. Most importantly, the bulk of the eyewitness testimony in the report concerning the events during that time was from the local Belgians who identified Wood from photographs after the war.

Wood's father, General Eric Fisher Wood Sr., was a member of Eisenhower's staff and a World War I veteran. In civilian life, he was a prominent architect in the Pittsburgh area, although he was best known for helping to found the American Legion. He was active in the National Guard and wrote a book on the ROTC program. Raised with a sense of service, Eric Wood Jr. had gone through Valley Forge Military Academy and subsequently attended Princeton prior to the war. He was married with two kids when he arrived overseas. A hard charger by all accounts, he became A Battery's executive just before deployment. The men of the battery respected him greatly and speak about him with reverence even today. Although there is a dispute on the exact nature of what happened, some facts are agreed upon. [110]

In the late afternoon of the 17th, Peter Mariate, a local villager, was

---

[108] Dupuy, *op.cit.*, 81-83

[109] *Ibid.*, 83, 150-154.

[110] Eric Fisher Wood Papers. Biographical History. Syracuse University Library Finding Aids. 29 Jan. 2013. http://library.syr.edu/digital/guides/w/wood_ef.htm.

out looking for a suitable Christmas tree. Even in the midst of war, traditions continued. He anxiously slogged around for some time in the desolate, yet still picturesque woods. The sounds of war still seemed far enough away. To his astonishment, he found two weary American soldiers standing in front of him. Speaking no English, the German-speaking Mariate tried to convince the wary Americans he was friendly. Facial expressions, hand signals, and bits of English words here and there finally convinced the freezing GIs to go home with their new found Teutonic rescuer. It was nearly dark, so they had to hurry. Upon reaching the village, Mariate welcomed them into his large, stone house and sent for a friend to translate. Mariate later told Army investigators that the man he identified as Wood was a "a big young man with confident, smiling face." [111] Wood apparently stated to the family that if he could not get back to American lines, he was going to fight the Germans behind the lines, conducting a war of his own.

The bold talk scared Mr. Mariate. He feared for his family's safety and pressed the men to stay the night. His wife offered copious amounts of food and warm drinks. Mariate warned them that the Germans were already overrunning the area. Escape was unlikely. The next morning, Wood and his companion were awakened, fed a hearty breakfast by Mrs. Mariate, and sent on their way.

The Mariates never saw them again. In the following days, small arms fire was heard erupting all over the forest east of the village. German wounded were seen being brought out of the woods. As the front line moved progressively west, Meyerode became a hub of German activity. The village hosted several notable figures, among them Generals Walter Model and Sepp Dietrich along with Belgian collaborator, Leon "Rex" Degrelle. Some villagers heard the Germans complaining about *banditen* harassing their supply convoys. Civilians were banned from the woods. German convoys inexplicably avoided the forest trails. Whispers among the townspeople grew louder with each day. [112] And a legend was born.

Initially, not everyone believed the story. One prominent member of Headquarters Battery strongly objected to the story and later wrote a history of the Battalion. The lack of American eyewitnesses added to his argument. No one who was part of this *guerilla-like* war ever came

---

[111] Dupuy, *op.cit.*, 151.
[112] *Ibid.*, 151-154.

RED LEGS OF THE BULGE

forward after the battle. Theories about who could have joined Wood abounded. Some felt they might have been infantry stragglers who had escaped encirclement on the Schnee. One officer thought it could have been members of a 106th ID Service Company who had been encamped near Meyerode on the 17th or escapees from the "Lost 500" on Hill 576. Adding to the mystery, the GI with Wood when he met Peter Mariate has never been identified by researchers, though he was reportedly an enlisted man. Many felt General Wood just used his influence to make his son appear in a better light. Regardless, Wood is still listed as KIA on December 17, 1944.

Although there is no doubt that the General wanted his son to be deemed a hero, in the opinion of this author and many other researchers as well as many of the surviving members of A Battery, Wood did conduct harassing actions against the Germans while the battle raged west of him. The evidence supports that theory. Army doctors determined that he was killed sometime in late January. This would have given him almost a month of surviving behind enemy lines. There was also no reason for constant small arms fire to be heard so far behind German lines at that time. The area had been overrun and secured by the 21st of December. And the Germans would not have wasted precious ammo on target practice. After the battle, Graves Registration reported that almost 200 bodies of German soldiers were found in those same woods, some hastily buried in shallow graves.[113] Additionally, the Mariates had no reason to make up stories. Lastly, all those who knew Wood personally including his fellow officers, said that his actions would have been in keeping with his character.

Lt. Wood was a dedicated, driven man. Major Goldstein had attributed A Battery's low casualty rate that first morning of the battle to Wood's diligence upon arrival earlier in the week. He made the men dig deeper, well-protected shelters near the gun line in case of sustained counter battery fire. Sitting still was not in his blood. Later that same morning, he bravely led five men, all volunteers, across an open field to a house he thought was acting as an enemy CP. Wood went in alone and thoroughly searched it, finding it empty.[114] During the first attack on A Battery's positions, it was Wood, and another one of his officers, Lt. O'Toole, who acted as the observers, helping to adjust fire on the

---

[113] *Ibid.*

[114] Report on the 589th Field Artillery Battalion by the War Department Special Staff, Historical Division. 23 January 1946. 106th Infantry Division Association 2005. http://www.indianamilitary.org.

assault guns. Some men are just driven to go above and beyond the call of their duty, no matter what the situation.

A small monument to the Lieutenant was erected by the local Belgians. It stands on the site where the bodies were found. The simple plaque is beautifully maintained by the villagers to this day.

A much less celebrated escape story began around the same time as Wood's. Just behind Wood's truck was the remainder of B Battery's personnel, with their commander, Captain Arthur Brown, in the lead. They had been delayed because of the need to disable the guns. Brown personally supervised the entire process, which didn't surprise his men. John Schaffner described his Captain as a leader *"par excellence,"* whose skill and attitude rivaled that of Eric Wood. A native of Yonkers, NY, Brown had graduated Duke University in 1939 and went to work for B.F. Goodrich for two years prior to the war. He enlisted as a private before becoming going to OCS. [115]

While crossing the bridge, a Panzer was seen hiding in an alley. A desperate Brown did the only thing he could do. He fired his .45 at the tank's gun ports at a distance of only thirty feet. Though a severe mismatch, it apparently spooked the crew enough so that they were late getting a shot off. The first round fired missed the truck. Brown then turned his attention back to the road ahead just in time to see Wood's truck get hit. He ordered his men to get out and head for cover. With his men running every which way, Brown headed up a hill in a different direction than Wood had. He made it to cover, where he found some abandoned GI clothing, including long johns. After deciding he was not being followed, he headed west. A group of cooks from the 423rd IR, oblivious to what had gone for the past two days, were picked up along the way. Several would accidently veer off at one of the many trails heading north never to be seen again. The small party was eventually led out by a sympathetic Belgian farmer from the village of Houvegnez, just outside the town of Stavelot. A grateful Brown and the remaining cooks from 423rd dodged a few groups of German soldiers, and made it back to Vieslam, the site of the new 106th HQ, where he met up with Elliot Goldstein. [116]

The farmer mentioned by Captain Brown was most likely Edmond Klein, who became well-known for helping the Americans during the Bulge. He lived in the vicinity and was personally thanked by

---

[115] Arthur C. Brown. "My Longest Week," www.indianamilitary.org. 106th Infantry Division Association. 2006.

[116] *Ibid.*

RED LEGS OF THE BULGE

Eisenhower himself after the battle. On the 17th and 18th, it is known that he helped two large groups of Americans escape encirclement. One of those almost certainly was Brown's. [117]

Not everyone from HQ battery was in that first convoy that cleared Schonberg. With his first harrowing day of combat behind him, a battered Randy Pierson, swollen nose and all, looked forward to heading west and escaping the German trap. There was one problem - he had been left behind!

Upon the alert from Service Battery at 0700, Major Parker had given the March Order west. Pierson began packing his gear and making the rounds as any diligent sergeant would do. When he was almost ready to go, he realized one of his buddies, Private Edward Brown, was nowhere in sight. Brown, in his late 30s, was old for an enlisted man. The men never really knew his exact age. He apparently had left a career as an architect and joined the Army, even though he had bad feet. He was popular with his fellow soldiers, and the guys helped him as much as they could during the tough training. [118] Somehow he got through it, but now time had caught up with him. Running to the now abandoned CP, the desperate sergeant bolted upstairs looking for "Brownie," as he was known. His buddy was in bad shape, almost catatonic and soaked from a cold sweat. Unable to awaken him from his state, and knowing the cold would most likely kill him, Pierson gave Brown a shot of morphine. With a heavy heart, he fled the building. Remarkably, the Germans found Brown alive, took him captive and he survived the war.

As Pierson got back downstairs, he was shocked to find everyone had left. The only vehicle still around was a jeep with no gas. There was a deafening silence until the squeaking sounds of tank treads began echoing everywhere. Pierson did the only thing he could do and started running up the road toward Schonberg. Within a few minutes, an ammunition carrier (3/4 ton Dodge truck) popped out from the woods far ahead of him and got onto the road at top speed. Managing to flag it down, he leapt into the back. The truck was loaded with infantrymen from the 422nd and a couple of other men from his Battalion. His

[117] Guy Lebeau. "Sad Souvenirs or life of the People of Stavelot during the winter of 1944 -1945." Center for Research and Information on the Battle of the Bulge, 11 February 2005, 1 October 2012. http://www.criba.be/.

[118] Samuel Feinberg. Samuel Feinberg T/5, 589th Field Artillery Battalion, 106th Infantry Division," 106th Infantry Division Association. 2008. http://www.indianamilitary.org.

new friend, Corporal Charlie Fairchild, was driving. [119]

After a stop to go to the bathroom and then another to plan strategy for getting through the village, it was decided that they would fortify the back of the truck with whatever gear they had. Believing the Germans only held the north side of the village, they took all their gear and placed it against the right side of the truck. A BAR man was placed in the passenger seat for extra firepower. While they were coming down the long winding hill towards town, mortars began falling. Mounds of dirt and hot metal fragments rained down on them. As the road leveled, Fairchild sped up. They made it through one intersection, and then another until finally encountering small arms fire at the third. The infantry squad leader told Fairchild to pull over behind one of the houses. Despite being the ranking noncom, Pierson gladly ceded command to a trained infantryman who could lead them out of this mess. Splitting up his men, Corporal Donaldson of Houston, Texas, covered the fourth intersection. He told Fairchild to start through as soon as he heard them firing. Nervously, the artillerymen waited in the idling ammo carrier for the signal. Donaldson yelled, "*Commence firing!*" and waved the truck forward. Fairchild gunned it across the street. Stopping just long enough to get the GIs back inside, he then sped off once again. [120]

During the firefight, one of the infantrymen was hit and had to be left behind, Pierson watched in horror as he was cut down:

> The whole action took less than thirty seconds. M-1s and Carbines firing, the BAR chattering, the vehicle vaulting, the Kraut's returning fire, and one of the men lying in the dirty intersection screaming, "I'm Hit! I'm Hit!" Before anyone could react, heavy German fire was concentrated on the body of the wounded GI lying in the snow. The sight was awful, blood flying everywhere, the now dead body shivering and twisting from the force of enemy bullets. Even though I did not know the dead soldier, watching the GI's body being ripped to shreds by the barbaric volume of German fire made me sick. The poor guy did not have a chance. Fortunately, he did not suffer long. [121]

---

[119] Pierson, *op.cit.*
[120] *Ibid.*
[121] *Ibid.*

RED LEGS OF THE BULGE

After getting out of town, mortars began falling again. The hot metal ripped through the air once again. One of the riflemen was badly wounded. Reaching the main road to St. Vith, they finally encountered the retreating Americans lined up in a huge traffic jam. With a wounded man, time was of the essence. It was not until 1700 hours that they finally reached the outskirts of St. Vith and got the GI to an aid station. The bedraggled group finally split up from there. Pierson and Fairchild met up with one of their officers, Captain Huxel, and were happily reunited with many of their comrades. But the situation was still precarious. The Germans were reported to be everywhere.

More than half the Battalion had now been killed, captured or were still trapped behind enemy lines. Colonel Kelly never did get C Battery loosened from the mud's vice-like grip. The howitzers were disabled and the men scattered. He attached himself to the 422nd later that day and was forced to surrender on the 19th. A large contingent of C Battery, including their CO, Captain Malcolm Rockwell, tried to escape encirclement on the 17th, but almost all were killed or captured.

For the remaining members of the 589th, the war continued to rage. The three surviving howitzers from A Battery along with crews from A battery, B Battery and Headquarters were kept on the move. Temporarily tapped to support one unit after another, they finally received orders to head for a village crossroads called Baraque de Fraiture, where the Battalion would cement its place in history.

Bleialf had been overrun by 0800 on the 17th. American and German dead lay strewn around the village; many clustered near the Church. The surviving defenders scattered in every direction. Around 0830, thirty men and three guns from the 423rd Cannon Company made it back to the regimental defense perimeter. They were immediately deployed around the command post, which was now under immense pressure. Cavender eventually had to move his CP back to the 3rd Battalion HQ to await a promised air drop of supplies. Division said it was supposed to be coming soon. [122]

After hearing about the troubles of the 589th while they tried to withdraw, Lieutenant Colonel Lackey consulted with General McMahon. It was decided that the 590th should tie in with the infantry up near the Schnee Eifel. After being on the move all day and night, they finally dropped trails in the wee hours of the 18th near the regimental HQ.

---

[122] Dupuy, *op.cit.*, 88-92.

By mid-afternoon, Col. Reid had decided the situation was longer tenable. He released the batteries of the 591st from their responsibilities in order to withdraw back to Berg Reuland. Hoover informed his battery COs of his preferred route of withdrawal, but it would be a harrowing retreat. They would run a gauntlet of German fire which included more of the dreaded *screaming meemies*. Thanks to determined counterattacks of the 424th infantry all day, the Germans were slowed, and the artillerymen made it back to Burg Reuland around 2300 hours. The entire Battalion was then ordered to push forward to Grufflingen. Once there, Ringer was given an onerous task, but one he was pleased to have. He would have to reconnoiter new positions to the rear and lead the Battalion out. Punch drunk from a lack of sleep, what little adrenaline Ringer had left was wearing thin. The motley collection of artillery units, infantry stragglers, American and German wounded, as well as German POWs got through to the town of Maldingen. Ringer's own Service Battery was down the road near Beho, so before long he was on the road again. [123]

Despite the atrocious weather that morning, the artillery liaison pilots continued to take off in search of German armored columns. Flying low, they were easy targets for German machine gun fire but several did manage to call in missions. The 592nd's 1st Lt. Alonzo A. Neese, Air Observer, and pilot, 2d Lt George Stafford, took off in an attempt to register the battalion on a point along the St. Vith-Schönberg road. Neese observed a column of German tanks and infantry on the road about thirty-five hundred yards east of the Battalion's new positions, just outside St. Vith. He adjusted the fire of Battery B on the column and observed in the first volley of fire for effect. The leading tank took a direct hit and blew up. The column stopped and dispersed. [124]

John Gatens' old battery commander, Lt. Graham Cassibry, went up with pilot Lt. Earl Scott, as his observer. They managed to get up to around 1500 feet but still took heavy fire. Scott got the plane down but with a lot of bullet holes. The next day they were ordered to evacuate the airstrip and get all the planes to Bastogne. The only problem was a lack of pilots. Lt. Cassibry, who had never flown an L-4 before, volunteered to take one out. He had washed out of pilot's training, but had 50 hours of flying time in other trainers. In heavy fog, the two men

---

[123] Ringer, *op.cit.*

[124] Lt. Col. Richard Weber, Commander, 592nd Field Artillery Battalion, December 10-31, 1944 After Action Report. Obtained from the 106th Infantry Division Association. http://www.indianamilitary.org.

nearly collided in the air. Having contemplated jumping, Scott decided to use his instrument training and spiral down out of the fog to find the ground. Both men landed in different locations in and around Bastogne. Cassibry came down almost in the City and spent the night in a nunnery. They met up the next day. Before long, their Odyssey continued. They flew north to find the 106th division HQ, finally ending up at Spa, Belgium. [125]

At Division HQ in St. Vith, the situation was chaotic. General Jones had been promised help from the 7th Armored, but they had to make their way south from Maastricht, Holland in bad weather. Their CO, General Robert W. Hasbrouck, had already arrived to confer with Jones. There was confusion from the start over what action to take and who would command the defense of the City. Jones, still hoping to save his two regiments, had been under the impression that help was imminent. He appeared to not know about the glut of American vehicles impeding the relief force. As the leading elements of the 7th Armored neared St. Vith, they ran into the traffic jam of frantic Americans trying to get away from the German onslaught. In some cases, their tanks pushed retreating vehicles off the road and kept pushing south and west. But the bad omens continued. Colonel Church Matthews, chief of staff of the Division, was killed when his staff car drove right into a German roadblock. His driver escaped, making it to St. Vith to give General Hasbrouck the horrific news. [126]

In the midst of all this chaos, were the civilians. They were now caught in the middle and faced vexing decisions. Some joined those units fleeing west. At first, it was just a trickle. Military vehicles got first priority for traffic, so many of the Belgians just walked along the side of the road, obtaining help from other locals along the way. Many still hesitated about what to do. Almost every family in the region had already had their young men conscripted into the German Army or into forced labor. Now that the Germans were back, their remaining children might be subject to the same fate. Other residents had lived through the occupation once before, and figured they could do it again, if the fighting did not come too close. The speed of the German advance shocked many, trapping them in their villages. Many villagers from Schonberg ended up nearby at an abandoned quarry in order to

---

[125] Earl Scott, "589th Field Artillery BN, Headquarters Company," 106th Infantry Division. 2006. http://www.indianamilitary.org.

[126] Charles B. MacDonald, op.cit. (New York: William Morrow and Company Inc., 1985) 332.

get out of the line of fire. Fear of reprisal suddenly became very real. The GIs forced Schonberg's Priest, Father Schumacher, to flee with them on the morning of the 17th.[127] Some even feared their own neighbors; there were civilians, mostly the ethnic Germans, still loyal to the Fatherland. The Germans considered this their territory and all the people in it, German. The area had been ceded to Belgium in the 1920s because of Germany's defeat in World War I. So those helping the Americans, or having the appearance of having helped the enemy, would suffer at the hands of the Nazis.[128]

For the 333rd, misfortune would continue. After being overrun, some headed toward Schonberg where they met their fate with B Battery of the 589th. Others went cross-country toward the 106th infantry regiments. A small group from their Service Battery and C Battery headed west over the Our. Late on the night of the 17th, eleven of the men made it to the tiny village of Wereth, just northeast of St. Vith. They were taken in by Mathias and Maria Langer. But a safe haven it was not. A German sympathizer in the village informed on them. Sometime later, a patrol from the *1st SS* approached the house, and the GIs surrendered peacefully. They were led out of the village to a small, muddy field. Over the next several hours, all eleven were tortured, beaten and finally shot dead. In January, an American patrol from the 99th Infantry Division was directed to the site by villagers. What they found was horrific. Legs had been broken. Many had bayonet wounds to the head. Even some of their fingers were cut off.[129] Remarkably, the Langers escaped any reprisal from the SS. Some have speculated that in exchange for the information, the man who betrayed the Langers may have extracted a promise from the Germans not to take any retribution on them. The Langers apparently knew who gave them away, but in a remarkable act of forgiveness, never revealed the person's name.[130]

No one was ever brought to justice for these crimes. Coming on the heels of the Malmédy Massacre, it went largely undocumented except for a couple of grainy photographs taken by Army investigators.

---

[127] Peter Schrijvers, *The Unknown Dead: Civilians in the Battle of the Bulge* (Lexington: University of Kentucky Press, 2005) 74.

[128] *Ibid.*, 6-8.

[129] "Remembering the invisible soldiers of the Battle of the Bulge." U.S. Wereth Memorial. 2012, 3 October 2012 http://www.wereth.org/index.php/history.

[130] Wouters, Carl. Email to Author, 5 August 2012.

During the investigation into Malmédy, the Army did review the incident. They determined that too much time had gone by to find the perpetrators who had most likely been either killed during the remaining months of the war or been discharged from U.S. custody since surrendering. The case was officially closed in 1947. [131]

For many years, the events surrounding the 333rd were largely forgotten. But the Langer family, and other devoted historians would not forget. Dr. Norman Lichtenfeld, the son of a 106th veteran, and the children of Mathias Langer helped form the U.S. Wereth Memorial Fund. The organization hoped to raise funds for a memorial. Their dreams were realized on May 23, 2004, when a memorial to the "Wereth 11" was formally dedicated near the location of the massacre. [132] Like Wood's, it is a simple symbol of sacrifice, placed where the bodies were found. The men have finally gotten their due. Recognition continues to come. Dr. Lichtenfeld is writing a book on the Battalion, and a TV movie about the massacre premiered in 2011.

The 333rd's A and B battery made it to Bastogne. They joined their fellow *Negro* unit, the 969th, and contributed mightily to that historic defense. While supporting the 101st Airborne Division, they suffered the highest casualty rate of any artillery unit in the VIII Corps during the siege with six officers and 222 men killed. [133]

The 17th had been a day of victory, defeat, escape, capture and death. Those west of the Our River had to stay on the move to keep from being rolled up in the German tide. For those still trapped up on the Schnee, time was running out.

---

[131] "Remembering the invisible soldiers of the Battle of the Bulge," *op.cit.*
[132] *Ibid.*
[133] Lee, *op.cit.*, 651.

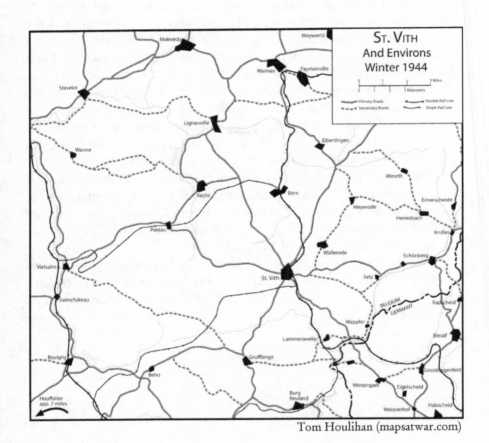

Tom Houlihan (mapsatwar.com)

RED LEGS OF THE BULGE

Chapter 3

18-19 December
The Ring Closes

W ITH the remnants of the 589th constantly on the move and the 591st and 592nd in a fighting retreat, the only intact artillery battalion left on the wrong side of the Our was the 590th minus its service battery. The entire Battalion had less than 300 rounds remaining as dawn broke on the 18th. [134] They spent the rest of the day in the defensive perimeter around the 423rd HQ. By nightfall, there would be just a few rounds per gun left.

The 590th spent the night of the 18th moving as close to Schonberg as possible. In theory, they were supposed to be able to support the infantry now amassing on the hills above the village. The reality was quite different. It was a tortuous and bewildering journey to nowhere that took them through their old positions at Oberlascheid. Pete House described the aimlessness of the past 24 hours:

> The 18th ended without further damage to our battery. It was move, dig in, fire, and quickly move. We were exhausted, hungry and cold. Cooks had not prepared any meals since the morning of the 16th. Then we received orders to get the vehicles running and move out. We spent the rest of the night in our trucks on a road in a valley—totally useless. Every so often we would move forward a little. I walked ahead of the driver so we would not run over anyone. He had poor night vision so I took over as driver. [135]

Eventually the Battalion ended up in a muddy field situated along the Ihrenbach stream. A crown of high hills surrounded them on three sides. Basically, they were at the bottom of a bowl and easy pickings for the Germans.

An oddly clear dawn broke on the morning of the 19th, and men

---

[134] Charles Whiting, *Death of a Division* (New York: Jove, 1991) 83.
[135] House, *op.cit.*

began to set up gun positions. It was the first day in quite a while without significant rain or snow. The men's last chance of escape, the infantry's thrust toward Schonberg, was about to begin in a matter of hours. They clung to that hope, but the daylight revealed the precariousness of their positions for Sgt.Hartman:

> When dawn broke we saw we were in a narrow valley. Steep, densely wooded slopes rose up on either side. There was swampy ground on our right front, and flowing directly across our path was a stream some six or eight feet wide. The infantry, unable to get its vehicles across the stream during the night, had abandoned them completely blocking our way. [136]

Lieutenant E.V. Creel, who had been a civil engineering student at Alabama Polytechnic Institute (now Auburn University), was A Battery's third officer. The "E" stood for Elnomac, the name of an Indian Chief who had saved his grandfather's life. He had been a member of the university's highly regarded ROTC program and somehow found time to be on the track team as well. Although trained as a forward observer, he never got to use those skills. [137] With the death of Captain Pitts, Creel and the battery's other remaining officers, Lieutenants John Losh and John S. Colman, were needed to aid Rex Rhoden. The men had led the battery for the past three disappointing days. The few rounds that were left were mostly smoke. Since the 16th, Creel had heard the agonizing calls between Rhoden and Battalion as Colonel Lackey and his exec, Major Meadows, tried to placate the new CO with promises of supplies.

Around 0930, the Germans made their final push. A barrage from German 88s and 105mms began to fall. The men scattered. Cries of *"Medic!"* rose up everywhere. Sgt. Hartman felt the hopelessness of the situation:

> Generally, there was a feeling of complete frustration. The howitzers were utterly useless for no one knew where to fire them. The machine guns were useless for the same reason, and for the added reason that they were on trucks directly exposed to the shelling and the enemy machine gun fire. There wasn't a

---

[136] Hartman, *op.cit.*
[137] Phone interview with E.V. Creel, October 2005.

RED LEGS OF THE BULGE

German visible from the floor of the valley and it was impossible to ascertain where they were firing from because of the terrific noise. [138]

Orders were given to disable the howitzers, and some of the men prepared to surrender. They quickly smashed their carbines and pistols to render them useless. House had already destroyed the two 610 FM communications radios with a pick axe. They had rarely worked and had become nothing but ballast. After disabling their guns, Pete House, Private Joe Krouse and Lt. Creel headed into the woods. They hoped to find help in order to escape. Within minutes, they happened upon a clearing where they ran into Lackey and Cavender. Permission was granted for them to try and break out. Bumping into stragglers along the way, the group expanded in size rapidly, much to Creel's dismay. The larger the group, the easier it would be to spot. It eventually grew to about 25 men. Amazingly, they walked for several hours without seeing anyone. In the early afternoon as they made their way down a steep, wooded ridge, a German 20mm anti-aircraft battery opened up, and pinned them down. Round after round ripped through the trees just above their heads. Three men were hit immediately, and it looked as though a slaughter was about to ensue. Creel grabbed his handkerchief, and bravely began waving it as wildly as he could. The Germans immediately stopped firing. Remarkably, Creel was unharmed. All of the men were rounded up, and there was the customary searching of the POWs. [139] Strangely, the Germans took no personal articles from the men. Pete House even got to keep his pocket knife. They were then put to work. House remembers when one of the men objected:

> Some of us were ordered to prepare the AA guns for moving. One American refused saying that it was against the Geneva Convention. The German officer pulled his pistol and shot him in the head. That's when I learned to forget the Geneva Convention. [140]

Creel, House, and Krouse, like so many other GIs, would endure over four months of captivity during one of the worst winters of the

---

[138] Hartman, *op.cit.*

[139] House, *op.cit.*, and Creel, *op.cit.*

[140] *Ibid.*

war. Toward the end of his ordeal, Creel would be a witness to one of the most controversial events of the war, The Hammelburg Raid.

Cavender, and his counterpart in the 422nd, Colonel George L. Descheneaux, were beginning to realize the inevitable. Two of the 423rd's Battalions had met stiff resistance as they made their way towards the village and suffered heavy casualties. The GIs of the 422nd stood fast in the hills above the Andler-Schonberg Road. The aid station for the 422nd was located very close to Descheneaux's CP. It was filled to capacity. Colonel Kelly was with him at the time, and the strain on Descheneaux was evident. Stretcher bearers carrying the severely wounded would go by and practically bring the colonel to tears.

After a German barrage killed one of his battalion COs, Cavender sent an emissary for surrender terms. Descheneaux did the same, much to Colonel Kelly's indignation. He begged the Colonel for more time to allow some of the men to escape but was flatly refused. Descheneaux felt a deep sense of guilt over the losses of his men. After that confrontation, Kelly witnessed the Colonel break down and cry. [141]

Approximately 6,500 men went into captivity later that day. Some continued to hold out. Groups from various units met up on Hill 576 and became known as the "Lost 500." Among them was an observer from the 590th, Sgt. Hank Donatelli and a wounded member of the 589th, Vernon E. Brumfield, one of the few survivors of C Battery. Donatelli, a Chicago native who had attended Drake University on a football scholarship, had been on the move with his observation team since the 16th. With his battalion now overrun, there was nowhere else to go. Low on ammo and food, the group hunkered down as the Germans set up loud speakers urging them to surrender. It got so annoying that a small group of the GIs snuck down to the bottom of the hill and put the loudspeaker out of business with a grenade. But the situation was hopeless. The group held out until the 21st, when they too were marched into captivity. [142]

Small groups of infantry did make it out. Lt. Ivan Long's Intelligence and Reconnaissance platoon (I & R) of the 423rd picked up survivors along the way and got across the Our almost intact on the 20th.

---

[141] Kelly, *op.cit.*, 14-15

[142] Dupuy, *op.cit.*, 148-150; Vernon Brumfield, "589th Field Artillery BN, Battery C, 106th Infantry Division." 106th Infantry Division Association. http://106thinfantry.webs.com/.

RED LEGS OF THE BULGE

They brought the news of the mass surrender to Division HQ. [143] Long's group was most likely the last to escape. By nightfall on the 21st, an eerie quiet fell upon the hills south and east of the Our River.

Even after the surrender, hard luck continued to plague the surviving members of the 590th. On December 21, Belgian-born Lt. Albert C. Martin, the Battalion Operations officer, who had been temporarily assigned to *DivArty* that first week and avoided capture, was directing traffic through an intersection in the vicinity of Poteau. Not all of the Divisional HQ battery had shown up yet at the crossing. Concerned, he and his driver, Private Koka, drove eastward to try and find them. As they passed just over the crest of a small hill, a German patrol opened fire on the two men. Martin was hit and fell out of the jeep. Wounded but still alert, he frantically waved at Koka to turn around and get help. The last sight of Martin was him engaging the enemy with his carbine. The Lieutenant's body was found days later surrounded by enemy dead. After the battle, his body was buried at a temporary American cemetery. [144]

Martin's story had added tragedy. He was an only child and his mother was unable to cope with the tragedy. Helen Martin would die in 1952 at a psychiatric hospital. Albert was the result of a union between Helen and a Belgian man she had met while working as a volunteer after World War I. They soon divorced and Helen came back to the states, where she met Mac Martin. Mac was a prominent businessman in Minneapolis, who was also childless. So he adopted Albert when he married his mother. In 1947, Mr. Martin, worried about the state of his son's body, requested his remains be cremated. Albert's ashes are now interred at the Henri Chapelle American Cemetery in Belgium (plot G, row 9, grave 30). [145]

By the end of December 1944, the 590th had suffered over 90% casualties since arriving on the line (killed, wounded or captured). During the reconstituting of the Battalion in March 1945, there were only 40 survivors remaining of the original complement with which they had arrived overseas, which included just six officers. [146]

---

[143] Dupuy, *op.cit.*, 146.

[144] Mary Jane Smetanka, "More than Just a Cross and a Name," Minneapolis Star Tribune 19 February 2008, 17 August 2011 http://www.startribune.com/local/west/15752132.html?refer=y.

[145] *Ibid.*

[146] Ringer, *op.cit.*

Chapter 4

Parker's Crossroads

ALL over the Ardennes since the attack had begun, small groups of GIs had been setting up roadblocks and pockets of resistance, which put kinks in the German timetable. The events that would occur at a place called Baraque de Fraiture, later known as Parker's Crossroads, was one such example of these bloody battles fought by small bands of determined men. Only in this case, it was a ragtag group of skilled artillerymen led by the indomitable Major Arthur Parker and the very feisty Major Elliott Goldstein of the 589th.

Baraque de Fraiture lay at an X-shaped crossroads and was the second highest elevation in the Ardennes at 2200 feet. It got its name from the village that lay a thousand yards to the northeast. The small cluster of dwellings there consisted of a large inn and a few farmhouses. The road coming from the east (Salmchateau-LaRoche Highway) cut into the main north-south highway connecting Liege, Houffalize and Bastogne. Farm fields lay all around interrupted by pockets of dense forests. Seizure of any part of the north-south route by the Germans could effectively cutoff the remaining units to the east around Vieslam. The junction offered good defensive positions due to the relatively flat and open fields of fire between the roads and tree line. [147]

After their escape from Schonberg on the 17th, the Battalion was joined by Service Battery of the 590th who had escaped the onslaught by hurriedly evacuating their billet at Heuem, just outside Schonberg. The 589th now consisted of the three firing sections of A Battery, the surviving personnel from B Battery and part of the HQ Battery.

The Battalion's movements over the next 48 hours typified the confusion that was reigning all over the sector. Their new odyssey began on the afternoon of the 17th. They were first ordered to set up a roadblock north of St. Vith in the Poteau area. By midnight they were back in St. Vith. Ordered to Bovigny on the morning of the 18th, they came under the command of the 174th Field Artillery Group (some would say *hijacked*). For the moment, the Group consisted mainly of the 965th, 969th and 700th Field Artillery Battalions. Tanks had been

---

[147] MacDonald, *op.cit.*, 541-542.

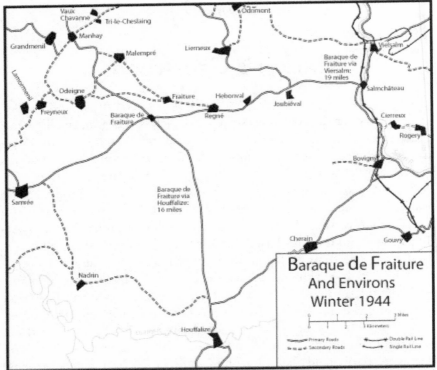

Tom Houlihan (mapsatwar.com)

spotted in the town of Charain, so the Group's CO ordered them to the nearby village of Courtil. That night when no tanks materialized, they were ordered back to Bovigny. It was here that the group was split up. The firing batteries, fire direction personnel and most of the officers were in one group with Parker. The other group, consisting of a portion of the 590th Service Battery and non-essential HQ men, were in the other. This group was sent back to Vieslam. For the firing batteries, the odyssey resumed at dawn on the 19th, when they were sent back to Courtil once again. Salmchateau was the next temporary stop. [148]

Finally, they were ordered west to the vicinity of Baraque de Fraiture late that afternoon, presumably to protect the flank of the

---

[148] Elliott Goldstein, "On the Job Training: An Oral History of the Battle of Parker's Crossroads and the Fate of Those who Survived The 589th Group," 106th Infantry Division Association. 1999 and "S-3, 589th Field Artillery Battalion After Action Report" (written by Goldstein), 31 December 1944. Both found at http://www.indianamilitary.org.

174th by setting up another roadblock. The Germans were supposedly in Samree, just to the west. Stopping about 500 yards from the actual junction, two of the howitzers were quickly set up to provide fire just in case a call came in for help. The Battalion bivouacked for the night. At this point, they were low on food and ammo, so Parker sent his trucks to Vielsalm for supplies. Fearing for the Battalion, General McMahon suddenly ordered the whole unit back for refitting, only to countermand that order just as quickly. Enemy tanks were in the vicinity once more. So the men were ordered to set up a roadblock the next day at the actual crossroads.

Regardless of whatever orders were to come down, both Parker and Goldstein were fine with staying put, no matter how dangerous the assignment. They had had enough of driving in circles and had decided on their last trip back to Vieslam that it was time to stand and fight. Parker realized the importance of this crossroads. [149] Armor and infantry support were supposed to arrive shortly, though no timetable was established. Buying time was about all they could do. As was the case for every unit during the first week of the Bulge, they had to fight a delaying action until a vengeful American Army could reorganize and strike back.

Parker was the Battalion S-3, and Goldstein, the Battalion Executive, but Parker assumed overall command with Colonel Kelly still listed as missing in action. Although the exec is usually in charge in the absence of the CO, both men just went where they were most needed. [150] The separation of duties and command structure were never discussed. The older Parker was highly skilled in artillery operations, and would be in charge of coordinating fire from a makeshift HQ. Goldstein took over perimeter defense. Both men were from the Deep South. Parker was an Alabama native and Goldstein hailed from Atlanta. Like so many in their position, they left promising civilian careers to fight the Third Reich. The 29 year old Goldstein was an attorney. Parker, nearing 40 years of age, had been a civil engineer.

The 589th still had a very competent core group of officers. Besides Parker and Goldstein, Captain Arthur Brown was back in his old job running the three howitzers that were left. The rough and tumble Captain George Huxel, assistant S-3, was still around, so was C Battery's Lieutenant Thomas Wright. He and one of his enlisted men had

---

[149] Goldstein, *op.cit.*
[150] *Ibid.*

made it to the Crossroads via Robert Ringer's 591ˢᵗ Service Battery. Wright had also been in Captain Brown's truck at Schonberg and had been initially captured with the rest of that battery. After noticing a very lax group of guards, he and many others escaped into the woods making it to American lines. [151]

Besides John Gatens, many other highly skilled enlisted personnel remained. Randy Pierson of HQ battery, using another one of his nine lives, was back for more. John Schaffner, one of the few survivors of B Battery; Frank Tacker, the Battalion Intelligence Sergeant; and Sgt. Barney Alford, one of A Battery's section leaders, were just some of the old faces that remained. Alford also brought along something to keep him occupied—a half-empty box of hand-rolled Cuban Panatela Cigars. As the days wore on, Alford's chief concern was running out of the hand-rolled delicacies, rationing himself to four a day. Some of the others included Gatens' section leader, Sergeant Shook, Battalion Master Sergeant Hill, Eldon Miedema, Harold Kuziema, John Rain, Charles Jacelon, Ken Sewell and Bernard Strohmier, one of B Battery's wire crew, and Calvin Abbot, of A Battery's wire section. [152]

After getting settled, John Gatens surveyed the scene:

> The weather was cold, wet and foggy with some snow already on the ground. Visibility was variable, clearing from maybe fifty yards to two or three hundred on occasion. I didn't even know who was in charge of the rag-tag group until I saw Major Elliot Goldstein out in the open, verbally abusing the enemy (wherever they were) with all the curse words he could think of, and at the top of his booming voice. I thought at the moment that he won't be around too long if there are any Germans out there to hear him. Apparently there were none, he drew no fire. [153]

He soon witnessed the results of being in close proximity to the enemy. A tank from the 87ᵗʰ Recon of the 7ᵗʰ Armored rolled up near a farmhouse. The crew jumped down and began milling around the house. Within minutes, one of the crew was shot between the eyes and fell dead. Captain Brown immediately ran over to Gatens, and ordered

---

[151] Arthur C. Brown. "My Longest Week," 106th Infantry Division Association. 2006. http://www.indianamilitary.org.

[152] Goldstein, *op.cit.*, and Pierson, *op.cit.*

[153] Gatens, "John Gatens, 589th Field Artillery Battalion, A Battery."

him to fire three rounds into the trees from which they all thought the shot had come. It must have worked or the sniper kept on the move. No more shots came from that area. [154]

A command post was hastily set up in the main house as daylight waned on December 20. All three guns were permanently emplaced within the perimeter. The Battalion's fire control equipment had been lost on the 17th, so Parker had to use a 1: 50,000 map with a safety pin for plotting. The gun crews used a monkey wrench to set their fuses. Before they could get settled in, a nearby unit called for a fire mission. The 87th Recon reported that tanks were in Samree again. Using the 87th's observer and their rudimentary instruments, two rounds were fired to bracket the target. Then Parker ordered two volleys for effect. The observer radioed back, "Mission Accomplished." The enemy apparently never showed, so no one could gauge the effectiveness of the fire. [155]

Mr. Henri Lehaire, the owner of the Inn and his family were still there that first morning. The property had been in the family since 1880. It was a tough decision to leave not knowing when they would be coming back or whether their house would still be standing. But with the sounds of battle edging closer, they were hastily preparing to move out. As Parker was setting up his CP, one of the girls came rushing in to look through one of the cabinets. Seeing her fear, Parker wanted to assure her. "You don't have to leave, we'll protect you," he calmly told her. Having survived four years of occupation, her survival instinct was too strong. "Boche come, I go," was her terse reply. She was gone seconds later. Mr. Lehaire would eventually stay on during the battle, and pay a heavy price. [156]

The men spent the rest of the damp, freezing day reinforcing their positions and trying to keep warm. Bit by bit, small groups from other units starting filtering through and were convinced by Major Parker to join the fight. Elements of the 203rd AAA Battalion showed up with their three halftrack-mounted quad .50 caliber machine guns and one 37mm gun. Then units of the 87th Recon actually moved into the perimeter just before nightfall. By late that night, more outposts were established, wire was laid for communication, and daisy chains of mines put into place along the roads. They did not have to wait long to

---

[154] *Ibid.*
[155] *Ibid.*
[156] Kelly, *op.cit.*, 124-125.

make contact with the westward bound Germans. [157]

John Schaffner and Ken Sewell, his fellow battery mate, were posted to a foxhole as observers on the outskirts of the southern perimeter. Around midnight, they started to hear German voices, the rattling of equipment and strange squeaking noises coming closer. The noise was from bicycles, and the Germans stopped just ten yards from their hole. They seemed to be lost in the misty labyrinth that was the Ardennes. Even in the darkness, the two Americans were able to make out the distinctive coal scuttle helmets of their enemy. A frantic Schaffner called the CP:

> I took the telephone and whispered our situation to Captain Brown. His orders were to, "Keep your head down and when you hear me fire my .45 the first time we will sweep the road with the AAA quad 50's. When that stops, I'll fire my .45 again and then we will hold fire while you two come out of your hole and return to the CP. Make it quick!" [158]

The AAA battery opened up, and it was a slaughter. When they heard the .45 again, the two men made a run for their CP and barely missed being shot by their own guys. Cries from the enemy wounded went on until almost dawn. At daylight, several dead Germans lay on the road. Apparently, enemy medics had pulled any still living ones away. It was later determined to be an 80-man patrol. [159] The battle had started and would not relent for the next 72 hours.

The 21st began with another attack by German infantry at 0630. It was repulsed, and fourteen prisoners were taken. Sniper activity continued throughout the day. Radio communication with Division had been spotty at best so runners had to be used. They were using an early form of FM radio and they were never properly calibrated. The feelings of isolation increased as each hour passed. [160]

At noon, word came down from Division via messenger to withdraw to Bra for reorganization. Parker realized that a withdrawal would leave the 87th and 203rd in the lurch. So he declined, or some would say, ignored the order. Herein lies the legend of the Crossroads. They would not abandon their comrades in arms, but would stay until

---

[157] Goldstein, *op.cit.*

[158] Schaffner, *op.cit.*

[159] *Ibid.*

[160] Kelly, *op.cit.*, 145.

reinforcements arrived. With no orders from the 3rd AD or 7th AD either, they were essentially on their own. Though no matter how much determination these men felt, it could not stem the anxiety that comes with the prospect that they may have to fight to the last man. Most of the men began feeling as if they were expendable.

That same morning, enemy tanks were reported near Samree again. Major Parker wanted Gatens' crew to get fire towards the village. The only problem was the gun was laid facing the northeast. The Major then ordered Gatens to get the gun turned around 180 degrees. The four-man crew wrestled the 5,000 pound 105mm howitzer to the right direction, but Gatens had to find an opening in the trees for a clear shot. Any shell fired would end up being rather close to the roofline of one of the houses. With complete faith in the calculations of Captain Brown and Major Parker, Gatens sighted the gun using his scope. It still seemed to close for comfort, so he then looked through the bore of the gun tube. Satisfied with that final look, a shell was loaded. Another check of the quadrant, and Gatens was ready. With fingers crossed, he ordered, "Fire!" It cleared the house. Three more rounds were fired, and the crew later found out that they did send those enemy tanks running for cover. [161]

At 1530, using the thick fog for cover, the Germans launched an attack directly from the east. Elements of the 3rd Armored Division (from *Task Force Kane*) arrived in time to help turn the tide. Unfortunately, not all the tankers could stay; but a forward observer from the 54th Armored Field Artillery (3rd AD), Lieutenant George Pratt, came in to help. Pratt was an experienced observer, and he helped Goldstein set up good zones of fire. He also had Goldstein reinforce one of the observation posts by throwing out all the furniture, smashing the windows and putting the mattresses against the walls below the windows. Word also came down that units of the 82nd Airborne would be coming to relieve them the next day. A squad from the 504th PIR came late in the afternoon and was sent immediately on patrol. They arrived back with ominous news. The Germans were digging in towards the east, and had set up a roadblock with discarded American trucks. Later that night, two 105mm assault guns, also from Task Force Kane, arrived. [162]

Ready for another long night, Randy Pierson entered the CP at

---

[161] Gatens, "John Gatens, 589th Field Artillery Battalion, A Battery."
[162] *Ibid.*

2000 to start his shift. Within seconds, an expressionless and exhausted Major Parker cornered him, Frank Tacker and Dell Miller. In a very deliberate tone, he summarized his concern, "I believe the enemy will mass troops, armor, and artillery along the Houffalize and Vieslam roads tonight." After a quick pause to let the gravity of the situation kick in, he continued: "We must be able to interdict and disrupt their assembly area." Then came the reason for this conversation. Parker sternly added, "To accomplish this, we must establish and man a forward observation post tonight. And I'll need a volunteer." Silence fell upon the group. None of the men spoke for a very uncomfortable few seconds. Parker repeated his request: "I need a volunteer who can adjust artillery fire." Out of embarrassment for the silence and in what seemed like an out of body experience, Pierson heard himself say the magic words, "Major, I will volunteer." He immediately remembered the old Army adage to never volunteer and began having second thoughts as Parker pulled out aerial photographs of the coverage area. Spending the night alone in a foxhole with what seemed like the entire German Army within arm's length, could break even the bravest of men. [163]

With his carbine, an EE8A field phone, and a hunting knife he bought before he came overseas, Pierson headed off into the unknown to look for a deep foxhole on the outskirts of the perimeter. He settled in for the night around 2300, checked his phone, and then waited. At 0130, vehicle noises began. The pitch blackness yielded no discernible outlines. Finally, he was able to make out just a tiny flicker of light in the distance. He rang the CP immediately only to be told to sit tight. Parker wanted more information before using up valuable ammunition. He checked in every thirty minutes, and there had been no change. At 0245, during one of his exercise breaks to stay warm, he made his way to the edge of the road. What he heard was frightening. Tracked vehicles were rumbling around and truck tailgates were slamming down. Infantry were being trucked to an assembly area and dispersed into the woods around him. It was time to find out how good his observation skills really were. [164]

The enemy was in almost total blackout conditions, so Parker recommended using white phosphorous shells to mark the target for Pierson. The brilliant flash lit up the black sky as the Germans began

---

[163] Pierson, *op.cit.*
[164] *Ibid.*

RED LEGS OF THE BULGE

to scramble for cover. Phosphorus shells can cause horrific damage. The molten fragments can burn right through a person's clothes and take off flesh. In a panic, the German drivers turned on their headlights, making Pierson's job much easier while bracketing the target. After a few adjustments, *(i.e. "Dell, try up 200, 200 Right, Change shell to HE, Fuse quick!")*, he called out something that every Red Leg loves to hear, *"Fire for Effect!"* Flowing with adrenaline, Pierson's next words sounded more Hollywood than Army, *"Hit them with everything you got...even the kitchen sink!"* [165]

The guns opened up, and he had a front row seat on the power of American artillery:

> Suddenly the still night was filled with explosions. Behind me the howitzers were firing rapidly and the target area in front of me had become an audible and visual mosaic of bursting artillery shells and multi-colored flashes. [166]

The CP wanted to know the damage in order to tell the batteries to stand down. But Pierson was more cautious asking them to standby. The Germans now knew an observer was close and they had to eliminate him. At a loss on how to proceed, Major Parker came up with a solution. The Major recommended firing a few rounds into the woods just east of Pierson's post. That would scatter any oncoming enemy swarm. After the first round, loud Germans voices were still heard nearby. The sound of boots crunching the ice-coated snow and branches snapping could be heard after the last barrage. A hornet's nest had been stirred up. *Wo ist der Amerikaner?* Assuming he was surrounded, Pierson could only think of calling out "Fire for Effect!" When Dell Miller called back to say it would mean tree burst directly above his head, he was undeterred: "Damn it, Dell, do it! Do it now! If you don't do it now, you can kiss my Southern ass good bye!" [167]

He dove down in the foxhole as deep as he could go, pulling down on his helmet. Immediately, explosions rang out. The ground shook violently. Tree bursts hurled branches through the air like spears. Hot, whirring metal fragments filled the air. Dirt and vegetation blew into the hole, coating Pierson with a thick layer of debris. Even with the eardrum-shattering noise, the screams of the enemy wounded were

---

[165] *Ibid.*
[166] *Ibid.*
[167] *Ibid.*

heard. Trapped among the trees, the Germans were now easy pickings. As suddenly as it began, the shelling stopped. The moaning and wailing of his enemy increased; it was a disturbing, but strangely comforting sound. An acrid, tear-inducing aroma of cordite and sulphur filled his nostrils. But the enemy kept coming. Boots were shuffling behind Pierson now. Whispering voices called out. Another fire mission was necessary. Dazed and shaking, Pierson grabbed for his EE8A, but it was gone, destroyed in one of the blasts. There was not even a sign of the phone line. He was on his own. Wrapped up in his own fatalistic thoughts, he felt for his knife sticking out his boot. After grabbing it, he waited. Within just a few minutes, someone was coming towards him. His grip became tighter. Then a helmet hit him on the shoulder. It was German! Seconds later a body fell into the foxhole and on top of Pierson. He heard the man grunt and could smell his foul breath. The man was still alive, leaving him no other choice:

> "My terrible fears suddenly turned into great strength and unleashed fury. The cold steel fighting blade was thrust upward with the power of both arms and legs. This thrust met the dead weight of the falling German body. The five inch blade entered the man's chest just below has Adams-apple, severing his sternum from top to bottom and in the process exposing steaming internal organs, and starting a fatal flow of his life's blood. Surprised, and in terrible pain, the German screamed, "Gott In Himmel!" The power of my upward thrust moved him completely out of the fox hole. With the German infantryman now lying on the parapet of the fox hole, I used the force of both arms to descend the fighting blade into the German's open chest and ripped toward his belly button. Only his metal belt buckle prevented the fighting blade from reaching its intended destination." [168]

Despite the deep stabs wounds, the man continued to thrash away at Pierson. Left with no other choice, he issued a *coup de grace* to his enemy, slitting the man's throat. One last gurgling breath and it was over. Germans were now everywhere, and with his phone shot up, all he could do was drop down in his foxhole, and use the dead body as cover. Sitting there in darkness, covered in blood, and smelling the

---

[168] *Ibid.*

man's innards was more than he could bear. As soon as it got quiet, he decided to make a run for it. Miraculously, the shaken soldier arrived back to the CP by 0430, where his buddies offered him copious amounts of brandy and cigarettes. [169]

Just before dawn on the 22nd, Parker ordered a preemptory barrage in order to disrupt any enemy that were inching up on the perimeter. It was a desperate move because the 105mm ammunition was nearly gone. He felt an all out attack was imminent again, but nothing happened that morning. Harassing fire continued all day as the enemy began infiltrating to the edge of the woods. The situation took a grim turn in the early afternoon as Parker, Goldstein and the other officers met near the farmhouse CP. In a momentary lapse in judgment, they met out in the open, giving the Germans a clear line of sight. Mortars suddenly rained down. One fell practically amongst the assembled group. Goldstein was thrown to the ground but unscathed. Parker was hit in the stomach and chest. Although conscious, he was clearly in bad shape. Still, he refused evacuation. A short time later, he lost consciousness, and Goldstein finally had him evacuated. [170]

Goldstein now had to takeover Parker's role as not only commander, but as cheerleader. He did his best to reassure the men that help was on the way. After all, the 3rd Armored Division was up the road, just five miles away at Manhay. Their tanks had already helped them out once, why couldn't they get here in force?

The loss of Parker from the CP was more devastating than anyone could have realized. Like Travis at the Alamo, he never stopped with his encouragement. Gatens remembers:

> Through it all Major Parker was everywhere, observing at the outposts, moving from place to place along the perimeter as one attack succeeded another. [171]

A company from the 325th Glider Infantry (82n AB) had arrived in the perimeter at 0300 that morning, with more supposed to follow. It was a rare bright spot during an increasingly grim 24 hours. Although small in number and short on firepower, their confidence was encouraging. They relieved the members of Task Force Kane, who had been ordered to withdraw. Most of the company was sent to the edges of

---

[169] *Ibid.*
[170] Kelly, *op.cit.*, 153.
[171] Gatens, "John Gatens, 589th Field Artillery Battalion, A Battery."

the perimeter, until they were forced back by heavy mortar fire. [172]

Back at Manhay, General James Gavin of the 82nd Airborne had grown extremely concerned about the situation at the Crossroads and along the main highway itself. On the night of the 22nd, he met with General Maurice Rose, commander of the 3rd Armored, asking what help he could send to the beleaguered defenders at the Crossroads. Rose flatly stated that his coverage area was so vast, he could not promise any help. He expected a German attack up and down the highway.

The Germans attacked again at 0430 on the 23rd. They were driven off. More prisoners were taken, including an SS officer. Lt. Huxel had been wounded in the early morning attack, but he decided to stay until ordered out. The pressure on Goldstein was becoming relentless. He knew this might only be a pyrrhic victory at best. Things took a turn for the worse that day as a detachment of the 643rd tank destroyer battalion, which had only arrived hours before, was captured. Their guns were used to fire on the men at Parker's Crossroads. [173]

There was a lull in activity as reinforcements arrived in the form of a company from the 509th PIR. The men had been sent at the urging of the 325th's CO, who feared being overrun any minute. Almost as soon as they arrived, the last of the telephone lines were cut by mortar fire. Goldstein now felt the time was right to speak with anyone who'd listen at the 3rd Armored Division detachment in Manhay. Maybe a high ranking officer would get more results. He decided to bring along his two prisoners as evidence of the grave situation.

Running the gauntlet, Goldstein made it to Manhay. The 3rd Armored's Colonel Richardson agreed to send a company of tanks and infantry to relieve the men. It was too little too late. They would never make it back in time. Goldstein got close enough to witness his men being cut to pieces and captured as the Germans' final attack began.

The attack began from the west and south ends of the perimeter. Enemy tanks now reached the crossroads. A couple of the Shermans managed to take out two *Panzers*, before the Shermans themselves started taking losses. Withering fire erupted all over the perimeter. Captain Woodruff of the 325th asked permission to withdraw when he

---

[172] Elliott Goldstein, *op.cit.*, and "S-3, 589th Field Artillery Battalion After Action Report" (written by Goldstein), 31 December 1944. http://www.indianamilitary.org. Copy of after action report was obtained from Carl Wouters.

[173] *Ibid.*

saw Tiger tanks beginning to ground up foxholes. Permission was granted. With the 325th pulling out, Brown, Wright and Huxel decided to shoot their way out of the perimeter as well. Wright led the first group out, but they were all captured. Brown led another. The men got away, although Brown himself was captured. The ailing Huxel got trapped at the main house with some of the men. Artillery and mortar fire began blasting away at the house. [174]

Amidst the chaos, John Gatens, who just prior to the attack had sent his gun crew to warm up at the nearest farmhouse, instinctively tried to gather his men. He dashed for the house. Before they could get out of the building, a round burst right near the door. Gatens was blown off his feet and sent flying to the back of the room. Others ran back to the cellar as the roof began to burn. By the time Gatens figured out that he still had all his body parts, a German officer was yelling for them to surrender. Two *Panzers* had driven right up to the door. Faced with certain annihilation, the men came out with the arms up. During the usual robbing of the new POWs by the SS, Gatens did notice one particularity: they did not take wedding rings. Whether it was out of superstition or respect for the sanctity of marriage, no one knew. It was nearly dark when Gatens and his fellow Lions began their march toward captivity. An icy wind was blowing. They now had no overcoats, gloves or wool caps. All that was left to protect them from the weather was a cold helmet and field jacket. So began their journey into hell. [175]

John Schaffner had also gone inside one of the buildings to get a brief repose from the cold. He made a snap decision as the attack started that saved him from captivity. Instead of running towards the cellar when mortars began blasting the house, he and Kuziema decided to make a run for the field across the road, where they ran into a drainage ditch. The attack was coming from the other direction, so they made another run for the trees. Kuziema was hit while getting up. Schaffner assisted his wounded comrade all the way across the field, where they saw the 325th infantry coming to their aid. Plunging into the deep woods, they all managed to get away. [176]

A small group, led by Sgt. Tacker, held out in one of the cellars for another day. The Germans never realized they were there. For the entire day the men heard the Germans going back and forth. One of the

---

[174] *Ibid.*

[175] Gatens, "John Gatens, 589th Field Artillery Battalion, A Battery."

[176] Schaffner, *op.cit.*

GIs became hysterical during the night and had to be restrained. RAF bombers came over the next day and pounded the area, narrowly missing the house. All became quiet and Tacker figured the Germans had moved on. He decided it was time to make a run for it. As the men exited the cellar, they were surrounded. The Germans had set up a battalion HQ right at the Crossroads. [177]

Randy Pierson and Barney Alford made separate escapes. Both made it to the relative safety of the woods during the final assault. Alford soon hooked up with a group from the 82nd to reach American lines. For Pierson, the adventure continued. Initially, he took off with Dell Miller. They became separated as they dodged the enemy machine gun fire and artillery. Things died down a bit and they met up again in the woods. They agreed to take separate avenues of escape. After a little while, Pierson ran smack into an enemy battalion HQ. After being questioned by an SS captain, he was put with a group of 82nd Airborne POWs. Pierson and the paratroopers didn't like the idea of being POWs and decided on a very risky course of action. As they began their march toward captivity, several men feigned illness, and others walked slowly. This separated the rear guard from his comrades. They eventually overpowered the German, and killed him. The men scattered in different directions and fled into the woods. Pierson ended up alone. On the verge of freezing to death after two bitterly cold nights of roaming around the Ardennes, he took refuge in a farmer's haystack. His peaceful sleep was abruptly broken when he heard footsteps. He cautiously peered up and to his amazement, saw Americans. He was saved; at least he thought he was. The tone of the GIs told a different story. [178]

An excited GI yelled into the breeched hay stack, "Raus, you Kraut son-of-a-bitch! If you don't come out with your hands over your head, I'll blow your fucking brains out!" With a voice squeaking under the stress, he yelled through his dry, cracked lips, "Don't shoot, I'm unarmed! I'm an American! I'll come out head first on my hands and knees." With equal emotion, the voice outside of the hay stack yelled, "You English speaking Kraut bastard, if you come out head first, I'll blow your fucking brains out. You better get down on your hands and knees and back out slowly, Very slowly, ass first. Do you understand me?" [179]

---

[177] Kelly, *op.cit.*, 175-177.
[178] Pierson, *op.cit.*
[179] *Ibid.*

The troopers assumed he was part of the Germans' deception campaign which was codenamed Operation *Greif*. Paranoia was rife among the Americans as rumors swirled about Germans in American uniforms causing havoc behind the lines. So Pierson got treated as the enemy and was threatened with being shot many times. The Airborne troopers took him back for interrogation. It took a day or two, but he was able to convince everyone he was a real GI.

In addition to the men from the 589th, there were 11 men from the 590th Service Battery at the Crossroads. Nine were captured or killed while only two escaped: Sgt. John Wagoner, who escaped with Captain Huxel, and Corporal Horace Duke, who was wounded and had to be evacuated. Wagoner went on to serve in the battery again under a new CO, Robert Ringer (formerly of the 591st). Transfers between the units became commonplace as they tried to piece the Division back together. [180]

The men of the 7th Armored and 82nd who were posted around the perimeter took heavy casualties as well. D Troop, 87th Recon, initially listed almost 50 men as MIA. The 203rd AAA Battalion had at least three men killed, with 14 missing in action and presumed captured. But 14 managed to escape. Two men from the Battalion attempted to escape after being taken prisoner and were shot. Of the 116 men from the glider rifle company, only 44 made it out. [181] Although around 300 men from the 3rd Armored took part in the battle, exact casualties for the 3rd AD's units are hard to determine since the situation was so fluid. But it's estimated that on the last day of the battle, at least five tanks and their crews were lost. Many more of their men were lost just outside the perimeter.

Mr. Lehaire was interrogated by the Germans on suspicion of helping the Americans. He was tied to a tree and left out in the freezing temperatures for hours at a time; in between he was beaten. After proving that he had helped a German pilot survive after a crash, they released him. Although he survived the war, he suffered the aftereffects of frostbite and the beatings for the rest of his life. [182]

---

[180] Ringer, *op.cit.*

[181] Statistics on the 87th and 203rd AA came the 7th Armored Division Association website, at http://www.7tharmddiv.org/baraque-7ad.htm and information about the 325th came from Richard Raymond's "Parker's Crossroads: The Alamo Defense," *Field Artillery*, August 1993, found at http://www.indianamilitary.org. Accessed September, 28, 2012.

[182] Gatens "John Gatens, 589th Field Artillery Battalion, A Battery."

The battle at Parker's Crossroads may have been lost, but holding out for four days against one of the crack units of the German Army bought time for units like the 3rd AD and 82nd ABN to regroup. For their exploits, the men were awarded numerous decorations. The unit itself received the French Croix de Guerre with Silver-Gilt Star for its defense of the Crossroads. Bronze Stars with a 'V' for valor were awarded to Elliot Goldstein, Randy Pierson and a member of the 3rd Armored Division, Major Olin Brewster. Barney Alford and Randy Pierson received battlefield commissions to second lieutenant. Purple Hearts went to Brewster, Brown, Kuizema, Miedema, Parker and Pierson. Abbott, Brown, Gatens, Miedema, Rain, Strohmier and Tacker all received the Prisoner of War Medal. [183]

Lieutenant George Pratt, the artillery observer from the 54th AFA, survived the Crossroads, but was killed in March 1945 as the 3rd Armored drove on Cologne. [184]

Horst Gresiak, a Battalion Commander in the 2nd SS Panzer, the unit which overran the Crossroads, commented to his American interrogators that Baraque de Fraiture was the most violent and toughest battle he had experienced during the entire war. Although later, *Obersturmfuhrer* Gresiak, in a face saving gesture, would claim that he had faced a much larger force, almost double the tanks and men that were really there. [185]

By January 1, 1945, only 92 of the original 504 men in the 589th were left. No better accolades could have been paid to the defenders than those written by General Gavin to Mr. Parker in 1980, "That stand your defenders made at the crossroads was one of the greatest actions of the war. It gave us at least a twenty-four hour respite, so I thank you and all the brave soldiers who were under your command for that." [186]

---

[183] Goldstein, *op.cit.*
[184] "George W. Pratt 26-42." Field Artillery OCS World War II Memorial. FA OCS Alumni Chapter. Field Artillery Officer Candidate School Alumni Association. 11 October 2012 http://www.faocsalumni.org/kiaww2.html.
[185] Gatens "John Gatens, 589th Field Artillery Battalion, A Battery."
[186] Goldstein, *op.cit.*

Chapter 5

Captivity

THE GIs who were captured during those first harrowing days of the Bulge began an odyssey of depravation that for some would not end until May 1945. Many of the thousands captured died of disease, malnutrition, and, in a tragic twist, Allied bombing. Although separated from their officers within the first days, many of the enlisted POWs stayed together after capture. This helped enormously with their survival. Sickness and hunger were inevitable. Having a buddy to rely on turned out to be essential because it might mean food to share or just someone to help you when you were sick.

The men were now *Kriegsgefangene* (German for prisoners of war) or *Kriegies* for short. The initial hours of captivity were traumatic. Getting over the shock of captivity was a difficult hurdle to overcome. Soldiers get used to following orders and not being the masters of their own fates; but now they were at the mercy of their enemy. As with everything else in war, their survival depended on a will to survive and a lot of luck. All of the men captured shared similar experiences and gained insight into the human condition under extremely trying conditions.

By January 1945, Germany's resources were getting scarce. POWs were last on the list of priorities. Just getting to a camp could take weeks. There were endless days in a freezing boxcar with nothing but a hole in the floor or helmet for a toilet; then it was a long, tortuous hike through the winter weather with very little winter clothing to protect one from the elements. During the next few months, their only food ended up being ersatz coffee, soup made of rotting potatoes or turnips and some kind of dark bread that contained sawdust. Once in a while, a dead horse was found and some of the meat would be used. A pig's jaw bone or ear might be added to the soup too. [187] Proper hygiene was impossible. Most of the POWs were liberated wearing the same clothes they had on when they were captured.

John Gatens was captured on the 23rd, days after the majority of his comrades in the 106th. His group of prisoners was a hodgepodge of

---

[187] House, *op.cit.*

men from different units; so he had few buddies. The next few days were spent trudging toward Germany over ground the Americans had previously occupied. He remembers a growing sense of dread with each mile as they were shuttled from one abandoned building to another:

> It now began to sink into our minds that the future was going to be horrible. I pictured in my mind that we would be placed in a camp some place with barracks and beds, mattress and blankets, regular meals and a place for exercise. What we got was cold, dirty, bombed out mills. Hundreds of men crammed into a space that is too small. [188]

The mood of the men began to change as well:

> Many things contribute to this. Being hungry and cold, and now a new problem started to develop, dysentery. In these buildings there were no bathroom facilities. You had to go outside in a big pit that had been dug for that purpose. Soiling yourself was now a big problem. You had to go outside, take off your under pants and outer garments, often including your shoes and socks, turn them inside out and try to wash them out with snow. Picture what happens now, putting on all the wet clothes and freezing to death until they dried up. [189]

When Gatens and the other men captured at the Crossroads reached Gerolstein, they were split up. Some went to work details near the railroad yard, while others were sent to camps. For all the men, Gerolstein was a nightmare. Many died of disease before ever reaching a Stalag. Already starving and sick from the long march, they now had to face the unremitting bombing of the RAF and USAAF. Prisoners were stuffed into old warehouses near the rail yard or stayed locked in boxcars for days. The boxcars were known as "40 and 8s" because they were meant to hold 40 men or 8 horses. The Germans forced twice as many men into the cars. There were no bomb shelters for POWs. All they could do was pray. The concussions of the blast were enough to shake the cars off the track. Bomb fragments ripped through their

---

[188] Gatens, "John Gatens, 589th Field Artillery Battalion, A Battery."
[189] *Ibid.*

wooden structures wounding and killing the prisoners. The writer Kurt Vonnegut, a member of the 422nd and a POW, vividly described this experience in his famous novel, *Slaughterhouse Five*. Most the guards had abandoned their prisoners, leaving them to die. In many cases, some of the smaller POWs crawled through small windows at the corner of the cars, got out and were able to unlock the cars. The men then ran for the nearest ditch. [190]

Every rail center in Germany was targeted during the last week of December to stop reinforcements from reaching the Ardennes. On December 23, 1944 there were 63 officers of the 106th Division killed in a bombing raid on the Limburg rail yards and prison compound, including two from the 589th. One of the bombs made a direct hit on the barracks. [191] So many of the men were killed prior to being registered as POWs that after the war there was a lot of uncertainty about the exact number of men who died in captivity.

Gatens eventually passed through three different Stalags and some big cites, like Cologne and Bonn. He finally ended up at a camp near Bremen, in northern Germany. Eldon Miedema and Charles Jacelon, who had survived the trek with Gatens, were transported to the camp in Limburg at the end of January. It had taken a month before they were registered as POWs.

Bernard Strohmier's experience was even more frightening. Upon reaching Gerolstein, he was taken to an old stone castle run by German intelligence and interrogated by an American-educated officer who had lived in Chicago prior to the war. Strohmier was offered the chance to join the German Army. Whether this was because of his German surname, he did not know. He quickly refused the offer, telling the German he was loyal to the Allies. So then he was given the opportunity to fight the Russians. After another refusal, the friendly banter ceased. The Germans stripped him of his jacket, shirt and shoes. Then they made him stand on the balcony in the freezing cold with his arms raised; for how long, he did not know. He survived this near death experience only to be sent to a labor camp near the ancient city of Trier, Germany. In the waning days of the war, he was moved several times. Prior to liberation by the 9th Armored Division, he had sur-

---

[190] Gifford Doxsee, Doxsee, Gifford, Communications Platoon, Headquarters Company, 423rd Infantry Regiment, 106th Infantry Division. 106th Infantry Division Association. 2006. Letter reprinted at http://www.indianamilitary.org.

[191] *Ibid.*

vived nine straight days without food or water. [192]

Hunger made the men perform desperate acts. Medic Hugh Fisher of the 589th, was in a column with men from the 333rd, and remembers marching behind a few of the black soldiers. He observed something rather unique:

> I noticed that the German civilians in the countryside were more apt to throw these soldiers something to eat, simply out of curiosity, as though they were animals on parade. As the order of the column reshuffled at various stops, I made a point to march directly behind one of the *Negro* soldiers to catch what food he might miss. [193]

Just the mere chance at food held hope for Richard Ferguson:

> We were so tired we found ourselves falling down and it made us wake up. One time we passed a field with sugar beets still in the ground. We ran to the field and ripped the beets out of the ground. We ate through the dirt we were so hungry. [194]

Along with hundreds of others, Ferguson would endure several moves during the first few weeks of captivity until ending up at a permanent camp. He was transported as far as the Polish border. He finally ended up at a *Stalag* just south of Berlin. After meeting up at one of the camps, Ferguson was able to spend much of his captivity with Richard Hartman. Together they obtained a rather curious contraption that made the food a little more bearable:

> In the last camp we inherited a wind maker from one of the permanent POW's. The wind maker was constructed from tin cans from Red Cross parcels. One can formed a housing where fins mounted on a spool and driven by a shoelace over a pulley arrangement forced air through a channel to the underside of a can with holes punched in the bottom. The forced air caused a blower condition which only required a few twigs to obtain a real hot fire. I guess we were fortunate to escape a real bad case of diarrhea since we were later informed by a guard

---

[192] Kelly, *op.cit.*, 222-223.
[193] Tyler Fisher, *A Medic's War* (San Diego: Aventine Press, 2005) 44-45.
[194] Ferguson. "Sgt. T/4 Richard C. Ferguson 31329406."

that the Germans used human feces to fertilize their potatoes. Some prisoners got dysentery so bad from eating potato skins that it resulted in death. [195]

Initially, a large majority of the 106th enlisted personnel and officers ended up in Stalag IX-B in Bad Orb, a mountain village in central Germany. Many arrived on Christmas Day. Far from being a picturesque alpine retreat, this was one of the worst camps in all of Germany. The camp already had hundreds of POWs from several Allied armies. During processing, the men endured long lines of waiting in the cold to get their picture taken. Then they were issued a work classification card and new dog tags that included their new ID number and the name of the camp. In early January, the officers from the 106th were marched off to the camp in Hammelburg. The two saving graces for the GIs was that the Germans left some of the 106th medical officers at the camp and even more importantly, the helpfulness of their Allies already at the camp.

Strange as it sounds, the long-term POWs, those Brits, and Commonwealth troops along with the French and Serbs, who had been captured during campaigns much earlier in the war, had an easier time than their brethren caught up in the Bulge. They had had time to come to terms with the shock of surrender, learned to survive, and prepare for the lean times that were coming. Most importantly, their bodies had gotten used to the less than stellar menu that was served to prisoners within the Third Reich. It is important to note that the one exception to all this was the treatment of the Soviet POWs. At most camps, they were kept separate from the other Allied POWs. They were treated as slaves for the better part of their imprisonment and millions died in captivity.

Many of the 106th enlisted men commented after the war on the amazing survival skills and organization of the British POWs with whom they shared the camps. The Brits pitied the new arrivals and welcomed them warmly. A large of group of men from the 106th arrived at Stalag IVB on December 30, 1944. The next night the British troops threw a New Year's Eve party, where they put on a show and introduced themselves to the Americans. Even after all that time in captivity, the GIs were amazed at their encouragement. "Don't worry, Yank, the *Jerries* are finished," was often heard by the new prison-

---

[195] *Ibid.*

ers. [196]

American soldiers never really trained to survive as POWs. Back in the States, they received training on how to escape just after capture, and there were some guidelines on behavior, but nothing of much help in their present circumstances. The American mindset was quite different from the British, particularly among the officers. Many of the American officers had been very successful throughout their young lives and to conceive of defeat was not easy. The individualism of the American character was not always helpful under these awful conditions. British POWs, on the other hand, made a science of resistance inside the camps all over Europe. Escape committees were organized, tunnels dug, and guards were bribed. They built radios and found other ways to get news from the outside. Everyone had a job and was expected to do his part. There was no stigma or shame attached to what they had to do. They were also healthier. Besides being used to the slim rations, they had been working on local farms, grabbing turnips and potatoes to supplement their meager rations. Exercise was not only encouraged, but considered a prisoner's duty.

Pete House was also fortunate to have a close friend with him throughout captivity, Utah native Raymond Brown. They were held at IX-B until liberation and their experiences are representative of life for all of the American POWs held in those last few months of the war.

After just a few days as a prisoner, House was amazed at what Americans took for granted back in the States; fresh water, lots of food, and clean clothes were standard for most Americans. Now as a POW, these items became a daily struggle to find. There were 250 men to a barracks containing triple decker bunks covered with burlap mattresses. The latrine was a room with a hole in the floor leading to a cesspool. [197] Water was a constant struggle:

> The only way to get water to our camp was to carry it in 55 gallon barrels from the German Officers quarters below the stalag. Four men could hardly handle one of these barrels. This water was strictly for the kitchen. No water for washing or

---

[196] Weldon Lane, "CPL Weldon V. Lane, Anti-Tank Platoon, Headquarters Company, Second Battalion, 423rd Regiment, 106th Infantry Division." 106th Infantry Division Association. 2006. http://www.indianamilitary.org.

[197] House, *op.cit.*

drinking. There was a concrete lined pond or pool near our gate. We began drinking from this. It is doubtful if we could have survived through April without water. [198]

Of course, food was the main thing on everyone's mind:

> At first we each received a small pat of margarine and either cheese, sausage, or marmalade with our daily bread. Gradually this was reduced until all we got was bread. Towards the end we had to share a loaf with seven then eight men. The last few weeks the bread ran out and we had two or three boiled potatoes each about 1 to 1½ inches in diameter. We figured we were receiving 1000 calories a day when we arrived and it dropped down to 500 calories towards the end. [199]

Under these stressful and freezing conditions, a person should have almost 2000 calories a day. [200]

Red Cross packages were supposed to be distributed regularly to all POWs. Raymond Brown secretly kept a diary of his time at Bad Orb and detailed the first day that the packages were distributed, January 31. Four men got a package with a variety of foods, and cigarettes. Cheese, chocolate and Spam along with eight quarts of powdered milk were all distributed equally. Distribution of the packages turned out to be a rare treat because the Germans were stealing them. Stashes of the packages, which were loaded with candy and cigarettes, were found all over the village of Bad Orb by the American Army upon liberation. [201]

The true nature of the Third Reich was really brought home to the men at Bad Orb at the end of January. Their captors decreed that all Jewish soldiers would be moved to a separate barracks. Estimates put the number of Jewish POWs in the camp at around 150 to 200. The Germans said that this was all in keeping with the Geneva Convention. To justify the order, they used the argument that since the United States practiced segregation in their own army, why was this wrong? These statements lulled the POWs into a false sense of securi-

---

[198] *Ibid.*

[199] *Ibid.*

[200] House, *op.cit.*

[201] Raymond Brown, "Diary of Raymond Brown." 106th Infantry Division Association. 2006. http://www.indianamilitary.org.

ty.[202]

House had a lot of friends among the Jewish soldiers, and visited them frequently. After about a week, he found them gone; so were about another 100 of the non-Jewish POWs who were identified as either "looking Jewish" or considered troublemakers. They had been sent to the so-called Stalag IX-C, but that was a phony name. The real destination was the Berga am Elster slave labor camp in east central Germany, which was part of the Buchenwald Concentration Camp complex. Approximately 350 men from Bad Orb and Buchenwald were sent there to dig tunnels to house ammunition. No one was meant to survive. Already starving, the prisoners were worked to death. They were steadily beaten with rubber hoses by civilian overseers from the German mining industry. Some were shot under false pretenses, like Morton Goldstein of C Battery, 590th. Goldstein was supposedly trying to escape when he was shot in the back by one of the overseers. [203]

House went 40 years wondering what happened to those sent to Berga. He assumed they had all died. At the 1989 Division reunion, he was astonished to find at least 46 had made it home. As a final insult, and something that became commonplace, justice never came for the perpetrators. After the war, the camps two chief overseers, Erwin Metz and Hauptmann Ludwig Merz, had their death sentences commuted to only five years imprisonment. Metz had shot Goldstein. Not wanting to offend German sensibilities and fight Soviet influence, murderers were getting off. The politics of the Cold War denied justice to the victims once again. [204]

The camp at Bad Orb was finally liberated on April 2, 1945. It was one of the first camps to be freed. In the almost four months they were imprisoned there, 34 GIs died and were buried at the camp. [205]

Pete House made it home by April 28. A grand homecoming it was not. Trying to get home to Jacksonville was quite an ordeal. After making it to Atlanta, he got rousted by two MPs who claimed he was in the wrong uniform. He had on no insignia and was still wearing his combat boots along with the short-waisted, *Ike* jacket. Somehow he convinced the MPs of his background and made the train. Upon arrival, it was another bus ride until finally reaching his parents' house at

---

[202] House, *op.cit.*
[203] Flint Whitlock, *Given Up for Dead* (New York: Basic Books, 2005) 147.
[204] *Ibid.*
[205] *Ibid.*

11pm. It would be many months before he was free of the Army. His discharge did not come until January 1946. [206]

John Gatens was liberated on April 28, 1945 by the Welsh Guards. He and the other POWs had to wait another agonizing day before leaving, but Gatens remembers that the troops could not have been nicer to all the POWs. They really bent over backwards to help them. Information had to be gathered about who they were and where they were going to be taken. The doctors also needed to examine all of the prisoners. The prisoners were warned not to eat too much initially. A large intake of food after so many months of deprivation could kill them. So crackers and a little soup was all they could eat for now. The next day the group was taken to Brussels where they were deloused and received their first showers in four-and-a-half months. Gatens ended up with a large number of the now former prisoners who made it home by summer, eventually ending up at Fort Dix, New Jersey. He took advantage of the opportunity to see his family and girlfriend after receiving a 60-day furlough. One of his brothers got leave at the same time and they were able to get to Times Square for VJ Day. Discharge finally came in November 1945. [207]

Ferguson and Hartman were freed by the Russians on May 2. All of the Bulge POWs were freed by May 7. Richard Hartman came home with a hernia and hepatitis, but like House, remained in the Army until January 1946. He had been teaching surveying to new recruits for the remainder of 1945 and the Army offered him the chance to stay and make it a career. Needless to say, he turned them down. [208]

At liberation, almost all of the men were emaciated. Forty to fifty-pound weight loss was not uncommon. Many were still sick with pneumonia and other related ailments, but freedom had a way of curing a lot of ills. The Army gave them ample time for recovery prior to sending them home; they slowly fattened them up before their families saw them. Numerous medical exams were administered as well. The men did have some lingering health effects throughout their lives. Poor circulation from frostbite and digestive issues were the most common ailments. By the early 1980s, it was estimated that the average lifespan of a POW was shorter than that of other GIs in World War II. [209]

For many, the physical problems healed. How they dealt with any

---

[206] House, *op.cit.*
[207] Gatens, "John Gatens, 589th Field Artillery Battalion, A Battery."
[208] Hartman, *op.cit.*
[209] Gatens, "John Gatens, 589th Field Artillery Battalion, A Battery."

mental scars was up to the men themselves. Psychological evaluations were still in their infancy and conditions like post-traumatic stress disorder would not become well known until after Vietnam. So for many the only treatment was to get on with life. Their determination to survive translated into success in civilian life and many went on to very stellar careers.

Regardless of the elation that many of the survivors felt, they knew their lives were permanently altered. That first group of POWs liberated in early April arrived at New York Harbor at the end of the month to be greeted by cheering crowds and curious reporters. Their responses to the reporters' questions were extremely forthright for the time period. Disregarding Army censorship, many spoke their minds. Private Robert Moore of the 422nd Infantry Regiment, the son of actor Victor Moore, stated flatly, "I don't think any of us will ever be the same again." Anthony Nicodemo, a Private First Class, was even more succinct. "My mother's going to see a different boy," he quickly retorted to an inquiry. [210]

---

[210] George F. Horne, "1,975 Arrive home from Nazi Prisons," New York Times, 29 April 1945. (Proquest via the King County Library System). 28 September 2012 http://hngraphical.proquest.com.ezproxy.kcls.org/hnweb/hnpl/do/result s?set = searchalleras.

RED LEGS OF THE BULGE

Chapter 6

The Hammelburg Raid

I N late January 1945, many of the officers taken captive from the
106th including Cavender, Kelly, and Creel, ended up at a prison
camp near the northern Bavarian village of Hammelburg. It was a
converted military training complex, and became known as *Oflag* XIII-
B (Officers' Camp 13-B). After their arrival, the camp was almost filled
to capacity. Conditions were bad and getting worse. The spirits of the
men were in disarray too.

At Hammelburg, it was the Serbs who were the longest serving
POWs, having been captured during Hitler's invasion of Yugoslavia
and Greece in April 1941. They helped the Americans enormously,
offering them items from their Red Cross Parcels and other tidbits that
they may have picked up while working outside of camp. The Serb
doctors also worked tirelessly to aid American medical personnel.

Death was always hanging over their heads. Men died of pneumonia and other illnesses. On February 5, Lt. John S. Colman of the 590th
died of pneumonia at the camp hospital. He was 35. Colman, a native
of Pawling, NY, was the only American officer believed to have died
of natural causes at the camp. But the small cadre of enlisted imprisoned in a nearby compound were hit hard by disease brought on by
the overcrowded conditions. [211]

In early March of 1945, two more officers arrived at the complex
that would have a profound impact on the prisoners' lives. Colonel
John K. Waters and Colonel Paul Goode, with a group of about 1200
POWs, had been marched west from Poland as the Soviets overran
Eastern Europe. They were then forced into crowded, miserable conditions at Hammelburg. Goode, a regimental commander with the 29th
infantry division, was captured in July 1944 at St. Lo in Normandy.
Colonel Waters, formerly of the 1st Armored Division, had been captured during the Kasserine Pass debacle in February 1943, where
Rommel's Afrika Korps handed the Americans one of their worst defeats in history. Waters was noteworthy for another reason; he was the

---

[211] Paul W. Cavanaugh, S.J. *Pro Deo et Patria*. Ed. Robert Skopak. Lexington:
Palmetto Press, 2004, 103

son in law of General George S. Patton.

Waters and Goode were both hard-driving West Pointers who were captured early into their combat careers. As a consequence, they decided to make their captivity a form of resistance. They were the highest ranking officers at their compounds. Strict military discipline was enforced. The men had to shave and keep the barracks clean. To Goode and Waters, it was the little things like maintaining your dignity which helped one continue to resist the despair of being a POW. Committees were formed, meetings held, and representatives picked for various duties.

Though exhausted and malnourished, upon arrival at Hammelburg, the two career officers began enforcing their ideas almost immediately. Colonel Cavender, the ranking officer, was quickly replaced by Goode, who established better relations with the camp commander, *Generalmajor* Gunther von Goeckel. Discipline had broken down amongst the 106th men since arriving at the camp. This was evident by their sloppy appearance as well as their attitudes toward their commanders, particularly Cavender. It got so bad, the younger officers refused to salute him. Many in both the officer corps and enlisted ranks in the 106th felt betrayed by their commanders because of the surrender. This resentment carried over into the camps. [212]

The changes helped enormously. E.V. Creel stated that the men made an immediate impact on the discipline of the camp. He called Goode and Waters some of the most impressive officers he had met during his time in the Army. [213] The 106th men appreciated their experience on how to survive as a prisoner and felt a renewed sense of camaraderie after just a few days. Shaving became mandatory as did the saluting all senior officers. This unified the Americans again. Army discipline had been restored and they were now a cohesive force, with Goode their spokesman. All in the camp knew the Germans were finished; it was just a matter of time. The biggest concern was whether their captors realized the war was lost, and could conceive of a future after the war.

By the middle of March, although things had improved, the camp was still a very dangerous place. Lt. Charles Weeks of the 423rd's HQ Company was murdered by a guard. He had been late coming back from the latrine during an air raid, so one of the camp guards in the

---

[212] Richard Barron, Abe Baum and Richard Goldhurst, *Raid! The Untold Story of Patton's Secret Mission*. New York: Dell, 1981. 73; 95-97.

[213] Phone interview with E.V. Creel, October 2005.

RED LEGS OF THE BULGE

tower put a bullet in the back of his head. He was just outside the door of the barracks. Witnesses stated that he had been walking with his hands in his pockets. Despite the danger of being shot, four lieutenants along with the Chaplain of the 422nd, Father Paul Cavanaugh, bravely ran outside and grabbed his body to render aid. Goeckel claimed it was a misunderstanding on the part of the guard. [214] It wasn't the first time this had happened. Back in January, Lt. George Vaream, a member of the 106th Reconnaissance Troop, was shot and killed by a guard during another air raid in January. [215]

Within the Allied High Command, rumors of horrific conditions for the POWs had been rampant for months. After the revelation of the Malmédy Massacre during the opening days of the Bulge, Allied officials came to believe that many long serving POWs might be executed before Germany surrendered. How many of the top brass believed this, no one will ever really know. Access to intelligence reports concerning POWs was very limited at that time and who knew what is still a subject of debate. For Patton, it became a pretext for a suicide mission miles behind enemy lines.

Neither Goode nor Waters were expecting a rescue mission of any kind. So on the morning of March 27th, everyone in the camp was shocked when the sound of small arms fire and Sherman tanks rumbling down the road started echoing around the camp. Lt. Colonel Kelly, like everyone else, ran out to see the commotion. It took several hours until tanks burst through the main gate. Then the POWs began scattering around. In the confusion, Waters was wounded by a lone German soldier hiding outside the gate. He was hit in the lower back and buttocks while he carried a white flag to meet the Shermans, which had been done at the request of Colonel Von Goeckel. Now partially paralyzed, he was carried back to camp where Serbian doctors saved his life. Task Force Leader Captain Abe Baum, of the 4th Armored, and Major Alexander Stiller, a Patton aide acting as an "observer," finally made it into the compound and immediately began to inquire about the famous prisoner. Cavender gave them the bad news: Waters could not be moved. Desperate, Captain Baum decided to see for himself. Sure enough, the doctors told him to forget about transporting Waters or any of the wounded. [216]

There was another glaring problem. The small force, which had

---

[214] Cavanaugh, *op.cit*, 102-104.

[215] Barron, Baum and Goldhurst, *op.cit.*, 76.

[216] *Ibid.*, 156-157; 163-166.

numbered about 300 men with 16 tanks (Shermans and M5A1 Light tanks), 27 half-tracks and assorted other vehicles, had lost almost a third of its strength. It had used up much of its gasoline in the drive through Bavaria to get there. They had covered over 60 miles in less than two days. Along the way they had run into determined opposition by ad hoc units of Germans, but also surrendering German soldiers and jubilant Russian slave laborers. Wounded had to be left along the route for the German Army to pick up. The dead were buried by German civilians. Now they had to turn around and do it all over again. Baum knew he could not hold out this far behind enemy lines, but felt compelled to help these long-suffering GIs. So he offered the POWs a chance to get on top of the tanks and ride out. [217]

Kelly was happy to be free, but did not like the odds of riding on top of a moving target in bad weather. Declining the offer, he obtained a compass and looked around for anyone else willing to walk cross-country to American lines. His former A Battery commander, Aloysius Menke, quickly concurred. Menke, as his name suggests, knew a little German, which would turn out to be a godsend. Their friend, Lieutenant Colonel Scales, a former Battalion CO in the 422nd, volunteered to go with them. Lieutenant Johanovic, one of their Serbian Army buddies, also asked to go along despite his poor physical condition. [218]

They immediately took off for the nearest swath of woods and planned to stay off the roads as much as possible. Within just a few hours, their Serbian comrade realized he could not make it very far. Four years of captivity had taken its toll. So he volunteered to go back to camp, but not before he emptied his pockets of any rations he was carrying, graciously offering them to his fellow prisoners. [219]

Starting off again, they walked for a day until they began to encounter a series of small villages. They made it through the first few as quietly as possibly. Late one night on the edge of a blacked out village, the three men were just inside the tree line trying to formulate a plan for getting through it unnoticed. The houses were spread out over large farm fields. Dense woods lay on the other side. They feared their luck was running out. Besides the villagers, there were the ever-present barking dogs, Kelly and the others sought another way around. To avoid it would have involved walking miles out of the way, adding

---

[217] *Ibid.*, 19-21.
[218] Kelly, *op.cit.*, 264.
[219] *Ibid.*, 265.

RED LEGS OF THE BULGE

misery to their already fragile condition. Menke came up with an idea. Instead of just creeping through the houses haphazardly, the three would march right down the main drag of the village in a small column similar to any other group of soldiers. In the darkness, no one would think twice. Menke figured the dogs are probably very used to the sound of boots in lockstep anyway. Marching single file, they stomped right up the street with hearts in their throats. There was no reaction from the populace, human or canine. After reaching the last house, they immediately dashed for the woods and cover. [220]

The next day they reached what might have been an obstacle too much for even these determined men. It was a fifty foot-wide river tributary with a highway bridge crossing. One guard stood on alert, pacing back and forth. Kelly, Menke and Scales spread out, searching desperately for another way across. Large boulders, a narrow point in the river, or even a large fallen tree would help. It was a fruitless search. The swollen river offered no respite from its freezing waters. There was no other way except right across the bridge. Kelly suggested charging the guard and overpowering him. Menke again came up with a plan. Bluff past the guard by telling him they were enlisted POW laborers from one of the numerous farms in the area and were lost. Kelly and Scales were doubtful, but agreed. Menke said if worse comes to worse, the two could tackle the guard while Menke went for the jugular. [221]

The Captain took the lead, carefully approaching the aged German with a relaxed but forlorn look on his face. He tried to explain using his hands and a phrase here and there. Behind him, Kelly and Scales acted nonchalant. They pretended to yawn, and look disinterested. The frightened old man let them pass, gesturing with his single shot rifle and they scampered away. About 100 yards away from the bridge, a shot rang out that whizzed over their heads. It might have been a face-saving measure. Diving to the ground, they crawled to the woods and safety. No other shots rang out, and they moved out even faster. After a couple of more days, with the food gone, Menke decided to go off on his own to either find the Americans or food, whatever came first. Luckily, he ran into men from the U.S. Seventh Army and he led them to the others. They were finally free for good. [222]

Kelly's friend Lt. Johanovic survived the last month of captivity,

---

[220] *Ibid.*, 267.

[221] *Ibid.*, 268.

[222] *Ibid.*, 268-269; 274.

and the two became lifelong friends. No other men of the 106th who were at Hammelburg during the raid are known to have made it safely back to their own lines.

The rest of the task force and the newly freed POWs, including Lieutenants Creel and Alan Jones Jr., son of the division commander, met fierce resistance on the way, which virtually destroyed the entire force just a few miles west of Hammelburg. Most were recaptured, and several suffered grievous injuries. Baum was seriously wounded and spent the next 10 days at Hammelburg in the POW hospital along with Colonel Waters. They were finally liberated on April 9. Waters was upset and embarrassed about the raid when he realized it was an attempt by Patton to get him out. He fully recovered from his injuries and went on to an illustrious Army career ending up a four star general like his famous father in law. Twenty five men of Task Force Baum were listed as killed or missing. Many men who were part of the Task Force claim the figure is higher. Approximately 20 of Baum's men managed to escape encirclement and make it back to American lines. [223] The secrecy surrounding the raid right after the war led to various inaccuracies in the official documents. Despite years of re-searchers working to piece together the real story and many of the survivors publishing their accounts, confusion exists to this day over the exact number of casualties.

For the long-suffering POWs, it had been too good to be true. They were marched back to their old barracks. Many were relocated to other camps within the next few days. Just as before, many would die from exposure, disease and Allied bombings. Goode and many of the others were sent to another infamous camp, Stalag VII-A at Moosberg, to sit out the rest of the war and would become witnesses to another famous liberation. Stalag VII-A at Moosburg was meant to hold about 10,000. It ended up with almost 100,000 by war's end. [224] The forced march to the camp became yet another horrific chapter in the prison-ers' experience. Amazingly, most would survive but some were not so lucky.

One of those was Lieutenant John Losh of the 590th. The Queens, New York native had survived several torturous months as a prisoner

[223] Charles Whiting, *48 Hours to Hammelburg: The True Long Suppressed Story of One of Patton's Boldest and Bloodiest Missions* (New York: Ballantine, 1970) 182.

[224] James H. O'Keefe, *Two Gold Coins and a Prayer: The Epic Journey of a World War II Bomber Pilot* (Fall City: Appell Publishing, 2010) 305.

until he was temporarily liberated during the Hammelburg raid. Ultimately, he too was recaptured and shipped out to another camp. During that march, his ragged group ended up at Nuremberg. Those in this group included Father Cavanaugh and Lt. Jim Keough, who was close with Losh. [225]

Nuremberg, because of its significance as a symbol of Nazi ideology, had been ravaged by RAF bombers for several years. Its train yards and manufacturing center were under constant threat. Bomb craters and destroyed buildings littered the area as a testament to the destruction. Upon arrival, the POWs were left out in the open not far from the rail center. As they lingered, air raid sirens went off. The German guards ran for the nearest shelters but the POWs were left to fend for themselves. At first, the prisoners were happy to have a ringside seat to view their enemy's destruction. That was until RAF bombers acting as pathfinders dropped flares directly over their position. The dark sky lit up like it was a new dawn. There were shouts to leap for the nearest hole. Father Cavanaugh gathered the men for the Act of Contrition. Then the Jesuit leapt for the nearest crater and covered his head with a blanket hoping the bombs would miss him. The ground rumbled under the deafening explosions and blasts of hot air hit the men. Sheets of flaming metal shards filled the air, and the wind generated by the blasts was like a hurricane. After the last bombing run was over, the men began to slowly raise themselves up. Moans and shouts were everywhere. Keough came running over to Cavanaugh. "It's Johnny!" he said. "He's been hit." [226]

Cavanaugh ran over to see Losh lying face down in the crater; but he was alive. Bomb fragments had hit him in the side, tearing through vital organs. A shirt was wrapped around his stomach to hold in his guts. Cavanaugh reached down and cradled his head. Losh asked Cavanaugh if he was going to be alright. No one really knew, but he assured the grievously injured officer that he would be okay. [227] Losh died a few days later at a hospital for British POWs, an indirect victim of Patton's hubris. John H. Losh is buried at Lorraine American Cemetery in St. Avold, France, Plot K, Row 49, Grave 19. [228] His widow,

---

[225] Cavanaugh, *op.cit.*, 144.

[226] *Ibid.*, 130-132.

[227] *Ibid.*, 133-134.

[228] "John H. Losh, 48-43," Field Artillery OCS World War II Memorial. FA OCS Alumni Chapter. Field Artillery Officer Candidate School Alumni
continued...

Isabel, would become a prominent member of the Gold Star Wives of America, even meeting with Mrs. Eisenhower on a visit to the White House in the 1950s. [229]

Captain Edward Luzzie, also of the 590th, lost a leg during the bombing in Nuremberg, but survived to return to his law practice in Chicago. [230] Both Keough and Cavanaugh survived the war. Fr. Cavanaugh returned to the U.S. where he continued his work as a Jesuit Priest before passing away in 1979.

The controversy over the mission will always remain. The death of President Roosevelt on April 12th overshadowed the failed mission and worked in Patton's favor. With correspondents distracted, any reprimand of Patton by Eisenhower remained in house for some time. Patton made various claims after the war about the real purpose of the mission. At first, he claimed that the chance of execution was too great not to try and he had no idea that Waters was at the camp. That is a dubious claim at best. The U.S. Seventh Army was on Patton's southern flank and just days away from reaching the area. Why would any commander take such a risk? Abe Baum always assumed that the only reason Major Stiller had gone along was to identify Colonel Waters. Patton also had access to intelligence via Ultra, the British program that broke the German codes. The locations of the camps and the movements of POWs were well known to the Allies. Details of that program did not come out until long after the war ended. He would have been forbidden to speak of that fact even after the war. Also, Third Army's intelligence staff was getting access to newly liberated or escaped POWs who were reporting the horrific conditions inside the camps. These reports must have played a role in the decision. The idea of his daughter becoming a widow so close to the end of the war must have weighed heavily on him and led to his rash decision.

...continued

Association. 11 October 2012 http://faocsalumni.org/kiaww2_files/loshjh.pdf.

[229] *Pittsburgh Post-Gazette*. February 23, 1953. This was a photo of Mrs. Losh at the White House while a member of the Gold Star Wives. Caption read "Callers," and featured her standing next to Mamie Eisenhower. News.google.com. 16 October 2012. http://news.google.com/newspapers?.

[230] Ko, Michael, "World War II POW Edward Luzzie, 90," Chicago Tribune 9 August 1999, 27 September 2012. http://articles.chicagotribune.com/1999-08-09/news/9908090041_1_prisoner-camps-artificial-leg-diary.

The proud general did admit one failure when it came to the raid. He did not send a large enough force. In one of his last interviews, he displayed his personal and official diaries to an Associated Press correspondent. This was supposed to show he did not know Waters was at the camp and that the raid had been conducted out of fear that the POWs could be murdered. Had Patton lived longer we might have gotten a more detailed explanation. With his death from injuries sustained in a car accident in December 1945, any chance of that was gone. [231]

[231] "Costly Prison Drive Explained by Patton," New York Times 6 October 1945. (Proquest via the King County Library). 28 September 2012 http://hngraphical.proquest.com.ezproxy.kcls.org/hnweb/hnpl/do/result s?set=searchalleras.

Chapter 7

They Fought On

A LTHOUGH the Battle would rage for another month, by the last week of December 1944, the Germans' timetable had been so utterly delayed that victory was now impossible. The Americans set up makeshift defensive positions around St. Vith, Bastogne and Elsenborn Ridge. They held out long enough for the Allies to regain their momentum. Patton turned his Third Army northwards, the British turned south and fresh units like the US 7th Armored were rushed to the front. Service and Supply companies were combed for infantry replacements and hurriedly thrown into the fray. Black soldiers were being recruited into the infantry to form segregated *fifth platoons* for many white companies. Most importantly, the skies began to clear, leaving the long German columns vulnerable to Allied air power.

Bit by bit, the salient shrunk. In the north, the 6th SS Panzer Army reached its limit by the 24th. Joachim Pieper had to escape on foot back to Germany as his namesake *Kampgruppe* was destroyed. [232] In the center, St. Vith eventually fell on the 23rd, but at a huge cost to both the city and enemy. That first week of the battle, General Bruce Clarke of the 7th Armored rallied the remaining troops, many of them from the 106th, to form what came to be called the *fortified goose egg*, so named because of the layout of its defenses. When British General Montgomery was given control of the northern sector by Eisenhower, he ordered the units to fall back, saving thousands of American troops. The city lay in ruins, but Manteuffel's Army had finally reached its breaking point. In the south, Bastogne held out in legendary fashion, refusing to surrender with General McAuliffe's succinct reply to a German surrender offer, 'Nuts!' The city never fell. Elements of Patton's Third Army would help break the encirclement by the 26th of December.

The toll on the 106th that first week had been near catastrophic. Whole infantry regiments and artillery battalions were gone. Almost eight thousand of the Division's complement had been killed, wound-

---

[232] MacDonald, *op.cit.*, 461-464.

ed or captured by January 1, 1945. Due to wartime censorship, details of the disaster did not start to appear in U.S. newspapers until late January 1945. [233] Many families had still not heard of the fate of their loved ones by that time. It would be March before many families received telegrams. For the remaining men of the Division, the final days of December and early 1945 would be ones of reunion, relief and retribution.

The 424th IR was relatively intact as was the 591st FAB and 592nd FAB. Division headquarters still existed but with a new commander. General Jones was felled by a heart attack on December 21, and the doctors had him evacuated. [234] His stress had been compounded by the fact that the fate of his son was unknown. He was a Battalion Operations officer with the 423rd IR, and was thought to be a POW. Like almost all other POWs, he was first listed as missing in action. That period of uncertainty between initial notification and an official notice from the War Department was agonizing for any parent. General Perrin took over temporarily. With just a few units intact, he quickly began to take stock of the remnants.

The survivors, many of whom just felt lucky to be alive, would endure several more weeks of fighting and live to see many of their former units reformed while others would move on to other units for good.

John Schaffner got back to the 106th on the 24th of December after spending a day with the paratroopers of the 82nd. Upon reaching the Division's bivouac, there were some trucks and personnel from the 589th in the vicinity. Miraculously, they had his duffel bag in the back of a truck, which he eventually brought home with him as a very treasured memento. At that time though, all it meant was clean socks and underwear. For the next two months, he was assigned to the 592nd as a fire control technician - a job he felt overjoyed to have compared with what he had been through that first week of the Bulge. The battalion saw some heavy fighting, helping to reduce the northern pocket

---

[233] "106th Division, in a 'Quiet' Sector, Took Shock of Nazi Break-Through," *New York Times* 22 January 1945. (Proquest via King County Library System). 27 March 2012 http://hngraphical.proquest.com.ezproxy.kcls.org/hnweb/hnpl/do/results?set=searchalleras.

[234] MacDonald, *op.cit.*, 125; 480-481.

After finally making it back to the 589th, Randy Pierson was promoted to 2nd Lieutenant. In an ironic twist, after almost being killed by his paratrooper rescuers while escaping the Crossroads, he was transferred to the XVIII Airborne Corps. He served with the 82nd and 101st Airborne Divisions as an observer until the end of the war. Eventually, he was transferred to the 3rd ID where he served in the Army of Occupation. He returned home a 1st Lieutenant in 1946. [236]

Jack Roberts did make it back to American lines; but like everything else, it was not easy. Upon setting off on their second escape the night of the 16th, Roberts and his two comrades found themselves immediately surrounded by advancing Germans and artillery, both American and enemy. But they still managed to get around the Germans positioned just outside the village, edging deeper into the forest. At first light, clad in olive drab, they were like sitting ducks silhouetted against the milky whiteness of the snow. Rain that had begun to fall overnight had now turned to sleet. As the swiftly advancing Germans kept to the roads, the dense woods turned out to be their best friend. By mid- morning of the 17th, they had come upon a small village which miraculously emerged from the morning fog. Cold and wet, the three desperate men needed shelter quickly. At the risk of falling even further behind the ever more distant American lines, they made the decision to rest. A few minutes respite from the weather, they argued, might save their lives. Finding a barn at the edge of the village, they sneaked inside to find a huge hayloft. It was the perfect place for drying off and hiding out. A German patrol soon sauntered up to the barn to take a look inside and get dry as well. Luckily they left after a few tense minutes without searching the place. [237]

Satisfied they were in the clear, the men started out again just before dark. Overhead, V-1 and V-2 rockets flew westward; their telltale exhaust lit up the dark sky. Flares shot by both sides also illuminated the way. They were still without sleep or a change of clothes. As they marched, the sights, sounds and aroma of battle were everywhere. The burning hulks of destroyed vehicles, German and American, littered the landscape. The frozen bodies of dozens of soldiers lay in their path;

---

[235] Schaffner, "Army Daze – A Few Memories of the Big One and Later Returns." 106th Infantry Division Association. 1995. http://www.indianamilitary.org.

[236] Pierson, *op.cit.*

[237] Roberts, *op.cit.*, 134-135.

their outstretched arms made for a macabre sight. They inhaled cordite and sulphur with every breath. Nearing the front line, Roberts found a Thompson lying next to a dead American sergeant. Armed with a real working weapon, he began to feel more heavily armed than he had with just the four hand grenades. Machine gun fire now rattled in the distance and the men strained to figure out who was doing the firing. Each step was carefully chosen to minimize noise. Hope increased as the firing became closer. Idling engine noise came within earshot. A yellow flare burst in front of them suddenly. It illuminated the tank they were hearing just long enough for Roberts to see it was American. They made a run for it, stopping just short of the American lines. Approaching cautiously, no one seemed to particularly notice the three men. After all they had been through, to be killed by a nervous GI would have been tragic. No one challenged them, so they began mingling among the platoon until they found an officer. [238]

After hitching numerous rides west, the three exhausted and frostbitten men found the gun positions of the 592nd on December 21. The men of C Battery were shocked at the sight of their buddies, but relieved. They were astonished at their miraculous story of survival. For Roberts, there would be one more surprise. He was made Chief of Detail and promoted to Staff Sergeant. Then his Captain made him an 'Acting Officer' which meant all the responsibility of the officer's burden without the title (or the pay). [239]

Over the next two months, as the counteroffensive gained steam, the 592nd displaced an untold number of times during the march into Germany, passing through some familiar places like St. Vith, Commanster, Werbomont, Manhay and Anthisneses. They provided support for various units, most notably the XVIII Airborne Corps. In one four day period alone, the Battalion fired 1850 rounds of HE ordinance. By New Year's Day, 1945, the Battalion had fired almost 5,000 rounds in nearly 750 fire missions. [240]

Roberts was later transferred to the newly reconstituted 589th, Battery A. He eventually received a battlefield commission to second lieutenant. After staying on for occupation duty in Austria, he made it home to Ohio in July 1946.

Robert Ringer's dangerous adventures continued throughout the next few weeks. He led one ammunition train after another, criss-

---

[238] *Ibid.*, 136-140.
[239] *Ibid.*, 143-148.
[240] *Ibid.*, 153-154.

crossed the fortified Goose Egg around St. Vith, and somehow avoided getting killed or captured. In fact, his whole battery was lucky. Between December 16th and January 25th, they did not lose a single man killed or wounded. Even when one of his trucks accidently drove into the middle of the Parker's Crossroads firefights, the crew stealthily avoided injury. Their efforts were not in vain. The 591st fired over 12,000 rounds of ammunition by the end of December, and Ringer's supply lines had hauled some 16,000 rounds.[241] The days of rationing ammo were long over. Like the 592nd, the Battalion stayed in the fight. The 591st was attached to the 82nd Airborne at the end of December. A short time later, they ended up with the 30th Division and supported the Division until the end of January. Eventually Ringer became CO of the 590th's Service Battery and the Battalion S-4 (Supply Officer) after the Division reorganization.[242]

After escaping the Crossroads, Major Elliot Goldstein found out that he and the remaining 589th men would be reassigned, at least temporarily, to other units. Goldstein became executive officer of the 592nd until April 1945 when the 589th was reconstituted. With the 589th back in business, and having fully recovered from his wounds, Major Parker assumed command of the Battalion. Elliot Goldstein was transferred back and took over as executive officer once again. Both men led the Battalion till the end of the war.[243]

The remnants of the Division were moved back to St. Quentin, France for reorganization. By April, the 590th, 422nd and 423rd were all reconstituted. They would all finish the war on the French coast awaiting the surrender of the German Naval Base at Lorient.

The 106th made it back to the U.S. in October 1945 where it was deactivated. The Army did reactivate it in 1948 as a reserve unit, but that would only last until 1950. The Golden Lion Division was no more, but a strong Division Association was formed and still exists today. Reunions are held annually and still widely attended. Many of the men have published their stories and spent their retirement years reflecting back on those harrowing days. There are memories both good and bad. That their wartime service affected them is an undeniable fact. To a man, they will tell you it made them better people, and the determination to survive made them successful in all walks of life.

---

[241] Ringer, *op.cit.*
[242] *Ibid.*
[243] Goldstein, *op.cit.*

Postscript

ARTHUR BROWN

While a POW, Brown was severely wounded during a bombing, and suffered a collapsed lung. Treated by both American and German doctors, he recovered, but the bomb fragment was not removed until 1958. After the war, he returned to North Carolina, working in the textile industry until retirement. Marrying while still in the service, he and his wife had 11 children and grandchildren. He spent his final years writing about his time with the 589th and POW experiences. Mr. Brown passed away in 1994.

E.V. CREEL

Lt. Creel stayed in the Army, serving in Korea and up through the Vietnam War, retiring as a Lieutenant Colonel in 1970. He began a second career in business, and eventually became a college instructor in the Tampa area. He and his wife Isolde, who he met in Berlin after the war, had four daughters. Mr. Creel passed away in 2010.

HANK DONATELLI

Mr. Donatelli went back to Drake University after the war and entered the insurance business in the Chicago area. He and his wife raised four children. He passed away in 2002.

RICHARD FERGUSON

With the help of the G.I. Bill, Mr. Ferguson went to college to become a mechanical engineer. He spent a decade working ten hours a day at a tool company and going to school full time all while married with two young children. Eventually, he rose to become the company's chief engineer and the position took him throughout the United States and Europe. Now in his nineties, he still hits the gym three days a week and works out at home the other four.

JOHN GATENS

After his discharge, John went to drafting and engineering school, eventually winding up in the aerospace industry where he got the opportunity to work on the Viking Mars Lander in the 1970s. Along with others from the project, his name was etched in a capsule on the craft. John and his wife had two daughters, five grandchildren and two great grandsons. He retired in 1986 and has remained active with the 106th Infantry Association since then.

ELLIOT GOLDSTEIN

Mr. Goldstein returned to Atlanta and went on to become a leading expert in the field of corporate governance, eventually expanding the firm his father started to Washington D.C. He remained friends with Colonel Kelly, contributing his story to Kelly's *The Fighting 589th*. He passed away in 2009.

RICHARD HARTMAN

Upon discharge, he went home to Baltimore. He eventually obtained a degree in English from Loyola College, and spent the next 39 years at AAA, rising to become Director of Public Relations. Mr. Hartman has written extensively on his experiences, and was interviewed for the Library of Congress' Veterans Project.

PHILLIP HOOVER

Colonel Hoover stayed with the 106th until deactivation and then remained on active duty. He retired in 1964 after 25 years in the service and relocated to Washington State. Mr. Hoover passed away suddenly in 1967 at the age of 58. He was buried with military honors in Enid, Oklahoma.

THOMAS PAINE KELLY

Mr. Kelly returned to his law office in Tampa, where he practiced till he was 92. He authored the book, *The Fighting 589th*. He passed away in 2008 at the age of 95.

HAROLD KUIZEMA

Mr. Kuizema went back to Michigan where he eventually took over the family hardware store, operating it until his retirement. He later served on the Board of Directors of the 106th Division Association. Mr. Kuizema and his wife have four daughters.

VADEN LACKEY

After his release from a POW camp, Colonel Lackey was sent home. By coincidence, his son Lt. Harrington Lackey, who had won a Bronze Star as an infantry officer, was on the same ship. Mr. Lackey became a coal broker in the Nashville area. He passed away in 1978.

ALOYSIUS MENKE

Returned to Ohio in 1946 and went into grocery sales for Proctor & Gamble. He and his wife raised three children. Mr. Menke passed away in 2011.

ARTHUR PARKER

Major Parker returned to Alabama after the war, where he resumed his career as a civil engineer. He passed away in 1983.

RANDY PIERSON

After coming home, he stayed in the Army Reserves while attending the University of Florida. He left law school to take a job with Southern Bell in Florida, but his life was interrupted again during the Korean War. Called back to service, he became an instructor at Ft. Sill for a year and was then shipped out to Korea where he served as an advisor to the ROK and a field artillery commander. After getting back, he resigned his reserve commission and took a job with AT& T Bell labs in New Jersey. Mr. Pierson passed away in 2007.

ROBERT RINGER

Mr. Ringer went back to work at Ohio State University, staying for 35 years, eventually rising to Associate to the Vice President for Personnel Services. He continued serving in the Army Reserve until

1972, retiring a Colonel. Mr. Ringer passed away in 2006.

JACK ROBERTS

Roberts returned home to work for General Motors, serving as personnel director for several plants and offices, retiring in 1986. He traveled back to the Ardennes during his retirement, and found the spot where he was ambushed. While gathering information to write about his wartime experiences, a WWII researcher based in Europe uncovered a photo in the German archives of the ambushed weapons carrier from his convoy that also showed the body of his friend, Howard Hoffmeyer.

JOHN SCHAFFNER

John returned to Baltimore after the war, first going into wholesale food sales. In 1956, he went into the defense industry and after 33 years retired as a computer systems analyst. In his spare time he became a pilot, serving in the Civil Air Patrol for over 20 years, retiring with the rank of Major. He and his wife have three children and six grandchildren.

RICHARD WEBER

Colonel Weber spent several years on occupation duty in Germany before coming back to the States as an instructor. While posted to the Pentagon, he worked at the Office of Unconventional Warfare, which included the Psychological warfare unit and the Green Berets. He and his wife raised two children before retiring in 1964. Mr. Weber passed away in 2002.

Appendix 1

The 106ᵗʰ Infantry Division

Major General Alan W. Jones, Commanding
Brig. Gen. Herbert T. Perrin, Assistant Division Commander
Brig. Gen Leo T. McMahon, Division Artillery Commander

INFANTRY UNITS

- 422nd Infantry Regiment – Colonel George L. Descheneaux
- 423rd Infantry Regiment - Colonel Charles C. Cavender
- 424th Infantry Regiment - Colonel Alexander D. Reid

ARTILLERY UNITS

- 589th Field Artillery Battalion (105mm) – Lt. Col. Thomas Paine Kelly [244]
- 590th Field Artillery Battalion (105mm) – Lt. Col. Vaden Lackey
- 591st Field Artillery Battalion (105mm) - Lt. Col. Phillip F. Hoover
- 592nd Field Artillery Battalion (155mm) – Lt. Col. Richard E. Weber, Jr.

OTHER UNITS

- 106th Mechanized Reconnaissance Troop
- HQs, Special Troops, 106th Infantry Division
- Military Police Platoon, 106th Infantry Division
- 81st Engineer Battalion (Combat)
- 331st Medical Battalion
- 106th Counter Intelligence Corps Detachment
- 806th Ordnance Company (Light Maintenance)
- 106th Quartermaster Company
- 106th Signal Company

---

[244] No relation to the author.

The Artillery Component of the 106ᵗʰ Infantry Division

Brig. Gen. Leo T. McMahon, Commanding Gen. Artillery
Colonel Malin Craig, Jr., Executive Officer
Captain Harold R. Daun, Division Artillery Headquarters

589TH FIELD ARTILLERY BATTALION (105MM)

Commander - Lt. Col. Thomas Paine Kelly
Executive – Major Elliot Goldstein
S-3 – Major Arthur S. Parker
A Battery – Captain Aloysius J. Menke
B Battery – Captain Arthur C. Brown
C Battery – Captain Malcolm H. Rockwell
Headquarters Battery – Captain Alva R. Beans
Service Battery – Captain James B. Cagle Jr

590TH FIELD ARTILLERY BATTALION (105MM)

Commander – Lt. Colonel Vaden Lackey
Executive – Major William H. Meadows
S-3 – Major Irvine Tietze
A Battery – Captain John J. Pitts
B Battery – Captain James R. Fonda
C Battery – Albert W. Henderson
Headquarters Battery – Captain Irving Chapnick
Service Battery – Captain Robert C. Ervin

591ST FIELD ARTILLERY BATTALION (105MM)

Commander - Lt. Colonel Phillip F. Hoover
Executive - Major Carl Wohlfield
A Battery - Captain Arthur Corcoran
B Battery – Captain Robert A. Likins
C Battery – Captain William C. Black

Headquarters Battery – Captain Bernard L. Lockridge
Service Battery – Captain Martin M. Dolitsky

592ND FIELD ARTILLERY BATTALION (155MM)

Commander - Lt. Col. Richard E. Weber, Jr.
A Battery – Captain Genero M. Mondragon
B Battery – Captain J. C. Gillen
C Battery – Captain Robert W. Smith
Headquarters Battery – Captain Bernard Richman
Service Battery – Bernard Weiderman

Killed in Action
for the 106th's Artillery Battalions

DIVISION ARTILLERY

T/5 Jack Noble

589TH FIELD ARTILLERY BATTALION

Pfc Perry G. Baker
Cpl Kilburn D. Camper
Pvt Kenneth H. Garrett
Pvt George E. Gaudette
T/5 Thomas H. Gilbreath
Pvt Wallace Goodwin
Pfc Thomas C. Graham
Pfc James T. Hays
MSgt. Preston Hill
Pvt Burton L. Hynum
Pvt Harold Keller
T/5 Kenneth R. Knoll
1 Lt. Ewing R. McCelland
Pvt. U.F. Mitchell, Jr.
2 Lt. Francis J. O'Toole
Pvt. Orvin R. Ristau
Cpt. Malcolm H. Rockwell
Cpl. Maurice E. Scanlon
Sgt. John A. Scannapico
2 Lt. James Semele
Pvt. Mike Skupaka
Pvt. Manuel V. Vanegas
Pvt. John Venmola
Pvt. Robert A. Wheeler
Pvt. Charles L. Wiseman
1Sgt. Leon J. Wochna
1 Lt. Eric F. Wood Jr.

590TH FIELD ARTILLERY BATTALION

WOJG. Claude A. Collins (warrant officer)
Pfc. Morton Goldstein
Pfc. Gordon F. Hustmy
1 Lt. John H. Losh
1 Lt. Albert C. Martin
Pfc. Ramon Meija
Pfc. Harold K. Mitchell
Cpt. John J. Pitts
Pvt. Carl R. Souilliere
SSgt. Norman E. Stone
T/5 Jack Tucker
T/5 William A. Waroth

591st FIELD ARTILLERY BATTALION

SSgt. Raymond H. Blackwell
Cpt. Edward A. Chateauneuf
2 Lt. Ronald J. Kaulitz
Pfc. Homer W. Miller

592nd FIELD ARTILLERY BATTALION

1 Lt. Isaac N. Alexander
Pvt. Lawrence A. Baker
Pfc. James T. Campbell
Cpl. Carl A. Himberg Jr.
Cpl. Howard Hoffmeyer
Pfc. Winfred C. Jenks
Cpt. Genero M. Mondragon
T/4 William F. Mouskie
Cpl. Roy Woodruff Jr.

Included in the men listed above, are those who were killed or died as POWs. Although the figures vary widely, the official estimates are that the entire Division suffered 544 killed in action or died later of their wounds in 63 days in combat. Approximately 180 died in captivity. Total casualties (killed, wounded, captured and missing) for the Division during the war were 8,647. 64 men were awarded the Silver Star and 325 were awarded the Bronze Star. Lt. Eric Wood was awarded the Distinguished Service Cross posthumously in 1947. (Information obtained from the 106th Infantry Division Association)

THE WERETH 11

T/Sgt William E. Pritchett
T/Sgt James A. Stewart
S/Sgt Thomas J. Forte
Cpl Mager Bradley
Pfc. George Davis
Pfc. James Leatherwood
Pfc. George W. Morten
Pfc. Due W. Turner
Pfc. Curtis Adams
Pvt. Robert Green
Pvt. Nathanial Moss

May they rest in peace

Bibliography

PUBLISHED BOOKS

Astor, Gerald. *A Blood Dimmed Tide*. New York: Dell, 1993.

Atkinson, Rick. An Army at Dawn: The War in North Africa, 1943-1943. New York: Owl Books, 2003.

Baldridge, Robert C. *Victory Road*. 1st Book Library, 2003. [Publisher's Note: This title was originally published by Merriam Press in 1995, in hardcover only. The author published a paperback edition through 1st Book Library, which merely reprinted the original Merriam Press edition. Merriam Press continued to offer the hardcover edition and in 2006 released the first paperback edition. New Merriam Press editions with improved formatting in both hardcover and paperback were released in 2012. Content has remained the same throughout all editions from both publishers.]

Baron, Richard, Baum, Abe, and Goldhurst, Richard. *Raid! The Untold Story of Patton's Secret Mission*. New York: Dell, 1981.

Cavanaugh, Paul W. S.J. *Pro Deo et Patria*. Ed. Robert Skopak. Lexington: Palmetto Press, 2004.

Cole, Hugh M. *The Ardennes: Battle of the Bulge*. United States Army in World War II: The European Theater of Operations. Washington D.C.: Department of the Army, Office of the Chief of Military History, 1965.

Dastrup, Boyd L. *King of Artillery: A Branch History of the U.S. Army's Field Artillery*. TRADOC and the Center of Military History, Fort Monroe, Virginia and the Center of Military History, United State Army, Washington, D.C. 1993.

Doubler, Michael. *Closing with the Enemy*. Lawrence, Kan.: University of Kansas Press (Modern War Studies), 1995.

Dupuy, Ernest. *St. Vith: Lion in the Way*. Nashville: Battery Press, 1986.

Eisenhower, John S. D., *The Bitter Woods: The Battle of the Bulge*. New York: Da Capo Press, 1995.

Fisher, Tyler. *A Medic's War*. San Diego: Aventine Press, 2005.

Hanford, William T. *Dangerous Assignment: An Artillery Forward Observer in World War II*. Mechanicsburg, PA.: Stackpole Books, 2008.

Kelly, Thomas P. *The Fighting 589th*. Bloomington, IN.: 1stBooks, 2001

Lee, Ulysses. *The Employment of Negro Troops*. United States Army in World War II: Special Studies. Washington D.C.: Department of the Army, Office of the Chief of Military History, 1966; reprint ed., Washington D.C.: U.S. Army Center for Military History, 1994.

MacDonald, Charles B. *A Time for Trumpets: The Untold Story of the Battle of the Bulge*. New York: William Morrow and Company Inc., 1985.

Peak, Donald T. *Fire Mission: American Cannoneers, Defeating Germany in World War II*. Kansas State University: Sunflower Press, 2001.

Pyle, Ernie. *Brave Men*. New York: Grosset & Dunlap, 1944.

Reith, John K. *Patton's Forward Observers: History of the 7th Field Artillery Observation Battalion, XX Corps, Third Army*. Richmond: Brandylane, 2004.

Roberts, John M. "Jack." *Escape! The True Story of a World War II POW the Germans Couldn't Hold*. Binghamton, NY: Brundage, 2003.

Shaw, Henry I., *First Offensive: The Marine Campaign for Guadalcanal*. Ann Arbor: University of Michigan Press, 1992.

Schrijvers, Peter. *The Unknown Dead: Civilians in the Battle of the Bulge*. Lexington: University of Kentucky Press, 2005.

Taylor, Hal David. *A Teenager's War*. Bloomington, IN: 1stBooks, 1999.

Toland, John. *Battle: The Story of the Bulge*. New York: Random House, 1959.

Tolhurst, Michael. *St. Vith: US 106th Infantry Division*. South Yorkshire and Conshohacken, PA: Leo Cooper/Combined Publishing, 1999.

Walsh, Edward V. *Serving the Pieces*. West Conshohocken, PA.: Infinity Publishing, 2008.

Whiting, Charles. *48 Hours to Hammelburg: Patton's Secret Mission*. New York: Ballantine, 1970.

—. *Death of a Division*. New York: Jove 1981

—. *Ghost Front: The Ardennes Before the Battle of the Bulge*. Boston: Da Capo Press, 2002.

Whitlock, Flint. *Given Up For Dead*. New York: Basic Books, 2005.

Zabecki, David T. *World War II in Europe: An Encyclopedia, Volume 1*. Routledge Illustrated Edition, 1998

Zaloga, Steven J. and Delf, Brian. *US Field Artillery of World War II*. Oxford: Osprey Publishing, 2007.

NEWSPAPERS, PERIODICALS AND ONLINE ARTICLES

"106th Division, in a 'Quiet' Sector, Took Shock of Nazi Break-Through." *New York Times*. 22 January 1945. Proquest. King County Library System, King County, WA. 27 March 2012. http://hngraphical.proquest.com.ezproxy.kcls.org/hnweb/hnpl/do/results?set=searchalleras.

Anderson, Richard. "US Army in World War II: Artillery and AA Artillery." 2000. *MilitaryHistoryOnline.com*. 29 March 2012. http://www.militaryhistoryonline.com/wwii/usarmy/artillery.aspx.

Bell, Raymond E. Jr. Black Gunners at Bastogne, *Army*, Nov. 2004. (elibrary, King County Library System, King County, WA). October 9, 2012 http://elibrary.bigchalk.com.ezproxy.kcls.org/ elibweb.

"Colman – Second Lieut. John Stark." *New York Times Obituary*. 12 June 1945. Proquest. King County Library System, King County, WA. 27 March 2012. http://hngraphical.proquest.com.ezproxy.kcls.org/hnweb/hnpl/do/results?set=searchalleras.

"Costly Prison Drive Explained by Patton." *New York Times.* 6 October 1945. Proquest. King County Library System, King County, WA. 28 September 2012. http://hngraphical.proquest.com.ezproxy.kcls.org/hnweb/hnpl/do/results?set=searchalleras.

Jones, Major Wilbur S. "Candidate to Officer." *Field Artillery Journal* 32, No. 12. (December 1942): 900-902.

Horne, George F. "1,975 Arrive home from Nazi Prisons." *New York Times.* 29 April 1945. Proquest. King County Library System, King County, WA. 28 September 2012. http://hngraphical. proquest.com.ezproxy.kcls.org/hnweb/hnpl/do/results?set=searchalleras

Ko, Michael. "World War II POW Edward Luzzie, 90." *Chicago Tribune Online.* 9 August 1999. 27 September 2012. http://articles.chicagotribune.com/1999-08-09/news/9908090041_1_prisoner-camps-artificial-leg-diary.

"Negro Artillery in World War II." *Field Artillery Journal* 36, No. 4. (April 1946): 228-229.

Pallud, Jean Paul. "Putting a Name to a Face." *After the Battle.* No. 144, (2009): 50-55.

Parker, Lt. Col. Edwin P. "Field Artillery Replacement Centers." *Field Artillery Journal* 31, No. 2. (February 1941): 83-86.

Reeves, Lt. Col Joseph A. "Artillery in the Ardennes," *Field Artillery Journal* 36, No. 3 (March 1946): 138-142; 173-184.

Smetanka, Mary Jane. "More than Just a Cross and a Name." *Minneapolis Star Tribune,* 19 February 2008. 17 August 2011. http://www.startribune.com/local/west/15752132.html?refer=y.

Thielen, Lt. Bernard, "Practical Method for Converging the Sheaf," *Field Artillery Journal* 29, No. 2. (March/April 1939): 126.

AUTHOR INTERVIEWS, LETTERS, PERSONAL NARRATIVES, DIARIES, UNPUBLISHED MANUSCRIPTS AND OTHER MISCELLANEOUS SOURCES

Brown, Arthur C. "My Longest Week," www.indianamilitary.org. 106th Infantry Division Association. 2006.

Brown, Raymond A., "Diary of Raymond Brown," www.indianamilitary.org. 106th Infantry Division Association.

Brumfield, Vernon. "589th Field Artillery BN, Battery C, 106th Infantry Division. www.indianamiltary.org. 106th Infantry Division Association.

Creel, E.V. Phone interview. 8 October 2005.

Doxsee, Gifford, Communications Platoon, Headquarters Company, 423rd Infantry Regiment, 106th Infantry Division. Letter reprinted at www.indianamilitary.org. 106th Infantry Division Association. 2006.

Feinberg, Samuel, "Samuel Feinberg T/5, 589th Field Artillery Battalion, 106th Infantry Division," www.indianamilitary.org. 106th Infantry Division Association. 2008.

Ferguson, Richard, "Sgt. T/4 Richard C. Ferguson 31329406," www.indianamilitary.org. 106th Infantry Division Association. 2006.
—. Letter to Author. December 26, 2010.
Gatens, John. Author Interview. 22 October 2011 (Fair Lawn, NJ).
—, "John Gatens, 589th Field Artillery Battalion, A Battery," www.indianamilitary.org. 106th Infantry Division Association. 2006.
—. Email to Author, 7 April 2010.
—. Email to author, 10 May 2010.
Goldstein, Elliott, "On the Job Training: An Oral History of the Battle of Parker's Crossroads and the Fate of Those who Survived The 589th Group," www.indianamilitary.org. 106th Infantry Division Association. 1999.
Hartman, Richard, "Richard Hartman, 590th Field Artillery BN, 106th Infantry Division," Library of Congress Experiencing War – Stories from the Veterans' History Project, 2004, http://lcweb2.loc. gov/diglib/vhp-stories/loc.natlib.afc2001001.00067/.
Hartman, Richard, "590th Field Artillery Battalion," www.indianamlitary.org. Reprint of article first appearing in The Cub, April-May 1949 edition, vol. 5, no. 5. 106th Infantry Division Association.
House, Pete, "My Experiences During the Battle of the Bulge," www.indianamilitary.org, 106th Infantry Division Association. 2006.
Lane, Weldon, "CPL Weldon V. Lane, Anti-Tank Platoon, Headquarters Company, Second Battalion, 423rd Regiment, 106th Infantry Division," www.indianamilitary.org. 106th Infantry Division Association. 2006
Pierson, Randy, "The Battle for Parker's Crossroads: Where an American Field Artillery Battalion Died," www.indianamilitary.org 106th Infantry Division Association. 2006.
Ringer, Robert, "My Adventures in Europe in World War II," www.indianamilitary.org, (Reprint of letters sent to Division Association). 106th Infantry Division Association. 2006.
Schaffner, John. "Army Daze – A Few Memories of the Big One and Later Returns.." 106th Infantry Division Association., 1995.
—. Email to author. April 20, 2010.
Scott, Earl. "589th Field Artillery BN, Headquarters Company," www.indianamilitary.org, 2006.
"The Limburg Bombing – Dec 23, 1944." www.indianamilitary.org. Reprint from The Cub, April-May 1949, www.indianamilitary.org. 106th Infantry Division Association. 26 September 2012. http://www.indianamilitary. org/106ID/SoThinkMenu/106thSTART.htm
Report on the 589th Field Artillery Battalion by the War Department Special Staff, Historical Division. 23 January 1946. 106th Infantry Division Association. 2005. http://www.indianamilitary.org. (Note: This report was a collection of after action interviews with men of the Battalion which included Majors Goldstein and Parker as well as Barney Alford, Graham Cassibry and Earl Scott. It was also used as a chief source of information

RED LEGS OF THE BULGE

on the last days of Lt. Wood.).

WAR DEPARTMENT FIELD MANUALS, TRAINING MANUALS, REGULATIONS AND ORGANIZATIONAL TABLES
(U.S. Government Printing Office during the War and Fort Sill, OK)

Field Manual FM *105-mm Howitzer M2 Questions and Answers* - Field Artillery School - July 1942.
Field Manual FM 6-40. *Field Artillery Firing* – February 11, 1942.
Field Manual FM 6-40: *Field Artillery Gunnery* – June 1, 1945.
G-1 (Rev.) *Time Firing Using Shell Fuzed with Fuze M54 or M55.* Field Artillery School (February 1943);
T-1 Organization of Field Artillery of the Infantry Division and Employment of the Field Artillery Battalion in Reconnaissance, Selection and Occupation of Position. Field Artillery School – November 1942.
Technical Manual TM 6-200. *Field Artillery Survey* – May 15, 1941.

AFTER ACTION REPORTS

S-3 After Action Report, 589th Field Artillery Battalion, 31 December 1944. Copy obtained from Carl Wouters. Report was written by Major Goldstein.
After Action Report, 592nd Field Artillery Battalion, for the period of December 10-31, 1944. Obtained from www. indianamilitary.org. 106th Infantry Division Association. Report was written by Colonel Weber.

INTERNET SOURCES

"7th Armored Division Troops in the Battle of Baraque de Fraiture, Belgium ("Parker's Crossroads") December 23, 1944." U.S. 7th Armored Division Association. 11 November 2012. http://www.7tharmddiv.org/baraque-7ad.htm.
Eric Fisher Wood Papers. Biographical History. Syracuse University Library Finding Aids. http://library.syr.edu/digital/guides/w/ wood_ef.htm. The site contains a biography of Eric Wood Sr.
"George W. Pratt 26-42." Field Artillery OCS World War II Memorial. FA OCS Alumni Chapter. 11 October 2012. http://www.faocsalumni. org/kiaww2.html.
"Dick Weber." Guardians of Freedom: The Nieman Enhanced Learning Center WWII Oral Histories Project. 8 November 2012. http://connections. smsd.org/veterans/dick_weber.htm.
Hunter, Captain Charles M. "History of the 16th FAOB and our experiences in the Battle of the Bulge." Center for Research and Information on the Battle of the Bulge, 11 December 2008. www.criba.be. 1 October 2012. http://www.criba.be/.

"John H. Losh, 48-43," Field Artillery Officer Candidate alumni website. http://faocsalumni.org/kiaww2_files/loshjh.pdf.

"John J. Pitts," University of Illinois Veterans' Memorial Project. http://www.uiaa.org/illinois/veterans/display_veteran.asp?id=67.

Laughlin, Kurt and Streeter, Timothy, S. "105mm Howitzer Ammunition: Boxes, Bundles, Tubes and Rounds." http://www. usarmymodels.com/ articles/105mm%20Ordance/1%2010. 24 June 2012.

Lebeau, Guy. "Sad Souvenirs or life of the People of Stavelot during the winter of 1944 -1945." Center for Research and Information on the Battle of the Bulge, 11 February 2005. www.criba.be. 1 October 2012. http://www.criba.be/.

Pittsburgh Post-Gazette. February 23, 1953 (photo caption). News.google.com. 16 October 2012. http://news.google.com/ newspapers? This is a photograph of Mrs. Isabella Losh (John Losh's widow) with a group of woman from the Gold Star Wives organization when they met with Mrs. Eisenhower at the White House. No article accompanied the photo that was captioned "Callers."

Raymond, Richard. "Parker's Crossroads: The Alamo Defense," Article at the 106th Infantry Division Association website. www.indianamilitary.org. 28 September 2012. http://www.indianamilitary.org/106ID/SoThink Menu/106thSTART.htm. This article originally appeared in the August 1993 edition of *Field Artillery*.

"Remembering the invisible soldiers of the Battle of the Bulge." U.S. Wereth Memorial. 2012. 3 October 2012. http://www.wereth.org/index. php/history.

Streeter, Timothy S. "Ammunition for the 155mm." Modeling the U.S. Army in World War II. www.usarmymodels.com. 20 October 2012.

"The Limburg Bombing – Dec 23, 1944." www.indianamilitary.org. Reprint from *The Cub*, April-May 1949, www.indianamilitary.org. 106th Infantry Division Association. 26 September 2012. http://www.indianamilitary. org/106ID/SoThinkMenu/106thSTART.htm.